MARY CHURCH

The story of a foundling

BY
SUSANNE HALL

St Mary's Church, Le Strand, London

MARY CHURCH
BY
SUSANNE HALL

The right of Susanne Hall to be identified as author of this
work has been asserted by her in accordance with the
Copyright, Designs and Patents Act 1988.

First published 2005 by Groundnut Publishing,
Gilray Road, Diss, Norfolk IP22 4EU
Tel: +44 (0)1379 652251

Editor: Ernest List

Typesetting and studio production: Eye Press Ltd

Printed and bound in Great Britain by
Eye Press Ltd, Diss, Norfolk.

ISBN 0-9527141-5-9

Cover Illustration: St Mary-le-Strand, London
Cover Photographs: Heacham village sign showing Pocahontas
and 2013243 WAAF Mary Church

Dearest Nanny,

*You wouldn't hear of me writing this during your
lifetime. But you always said that 'when anything
happens to me' I could do so. Well it has, and I will. Since
you died, the loss is entirely mine, not yours. As you said
'I'm ready to go, I've had a good innings haven't I?'
Eighty-nine years to be exact, and all of them as far as I
can ascertain, devoted to other people. It was our good
fortune that the last forty-three of them were shared with
my family. When, after 29 years with us, you divulged the
secret which had caused you so much anguish all your
life, I was stunned. It was such a poignant story, which
struck me deeply then as it still does today. I must try to
do justice to it and to you, the remarkable lady who was
the best friend that I could ever have wished for, who died
on January 30th 2004.*

ACKNOWLEDGEMENTS

As I read the acknowledgements in other people's books, I wonder at the efficiency of authors who keep lists, even as I wonder whose names they might have inadvertently missed. A minefield me thinks. I will avoid such a hazard. Of course I am grateful to all the many people who have helped me chart the life of Mary Church. All of them are named either on the cover of this book or within it.

But I must recognise the part that my children Mark, Alice and Jeremy played in the story. How grateful their parents, Tom and I were, that their behaviour never caused their Nanny to disappear into the distance on her Lambretta, but rather to remain as part of our family long enough to know, and sometimes even look after their children.

To my patient, bookaholic husband Kit Chalcraft, for reading and re-reading my jottings when other tempting tomes remained unopened on his desk, I say thank you.

Name	Mary Church
Place of birth	unknown
Date of birth	Presumed 30.10.1914

So reads the early passport of a nobody. Except that this particular nobody became a somebody who was loved and revered by all who were privileged to call her 'Nanny'. This is in many ways a sad tale of how the lack of a birth certificate, and the possibility of illegitimacy in the early part of the last century, could so blight a life. It is also a testament to a lady who, blessed with so little herself, was able to bestow so much love and care on those who were lucky enough to be her charges. It was to be twenty-nine years before she divulged her lifelong secret to me. Her real name was not Mary Church.

It was in 1960, when old-fashioned English Nannies were already an endangered species that I had three replies to an advertisement that I had put in the local paper for a nanny for our toddler son and the baby that I was expecting. One, aged 46, hoped I would not ask for too many references as she only had three.

"You see, I stayed with each of my families for such a long time. But if you'd like to ring up my present employer Mrs Ashworth I think she will speak well of me". She did. "Nanny?" said Mrs Ashworth, "She's a gem. James will be heartbroken when he knows she's leaving

5

because she's looked after him for 9 years, as well as his brother and sister, but now that he's going to boarding school we've no need of a nanny. You'll be very happy with her. She doesn't make friends easily and likes to keep herself to herself, and have the nursery as her own. But children adore her and she's wonderful with them".

Days later Mary Church came to see us at Rockland St Mary. I don't know what I expected but it certainly wasn't the lady walking across the lawn to meet me clad in motorbike gear, a crash lid under her arm. For a start I hadn't expected that she'd be doing the 30-mile journey on a Lambretta scooter. Indeed I didn't know she had such a thing. But there she was with her open face devoid of make-up, framed in her grey hair. She had clear blue eyes and gappy front teeth. My incredulity must have prompted her to explain that she was a WAAF mechanic in the war and a balloon operator. So she understood motorbikes. This had to bode well, as being the possessor of a Mini with starting problems perhaps I would cope with the children while she lifted the bonnet. It was also the defining moment for Tom my husband, whose forte was certainly not interviewing nannies. He had been persuaded and needed to hear no more.

A somewhat stilted conversation ensued as I asked her about her family and about the children that she had looked after and she asked me about our requirements. What would she like to be called I enquired? "Oh, I'm Nanny to all my families, Madam". Surely she wasn't going to call us Sir and Madam. Indeed she was and my protestations were met with, "Well that's what I've always been used to". I remember having misgivings that we rather than she might not come up to expectations. She explained that she had been brought up in Norfolk and as she still had an elderly aunt in Snettisham who she cared for, she wanted to stay in the county. Our toddler was introduced and immediately referred to as 'dare.' She did not seem to have a Norfolk accent but the three giveaway words were then and remained 'dare' for 'dear', 'noo' for 'new' and 'neffoo' for 'nephew.'

We liked her. She seemed unstuffy, was long legged and agile with tiny feet sensibly shod, and quite willing to turn her hand to whatever was required. "But I'm not much of a cook unless I have to do it occasionally". Indeed she wasn't as we later discovered, but then we were not looking for a chef.

To my astonishment, this seeming paragon wished to take the job and asked for £3 per week and one day off "after I've got the children up and given them their breakfast of course". That seemed some deal.

We upped it to £3.10 shillings and the future was settled. Today I suppose it would be £300 a week, all evenings and weekends off as well as a car and no domestic chores.

I've so often looked back on that day to see if there was anything that I might have missed and I'm sure there was not. Mary Church seemed, and continued to seem for the next 29 years, the epitome of a warm and generous personality whose own family background and upbringing, of which we knew comparatively little, had been that of the archetypal rural village child. How wrong I was.

Weeks later, when James Ashworth had gone away to school, I took our horsebox to collect Nanny from Stibbard in West Norfolk with all her worldly goods – her Lambretta, a bicycle, a trunk, a sewing machine, lamp and wastepaper basket. She was tearful, the goodbyes were ghastly for her and we drove home in near silence rather than false cheer. She had already said goodbye to James. She had known, but he had not, that his nanny would not be there to greet him on his return. She'd not be running any more races with him, nor would they be off together on bike rides round the farm. She would simply not exist in his life any more, after those nine happy years together. She had assured him that he would be happy at school. She'd sewn

James Ashworth (1958)

7

nametapes on all his clothes, packed his trunk with his new uniform and into his tuckbox she'd secreted an extra packet of sweets. She told me that she had done it all in the evenings when James was in bed. She wouldn't have liked him to see her upset - that would never do. The protective instinct of a parent was one I was familiar with. That of a Nanny seemed particularly sad, for whereas no one decreed that our children must move on and away from us their parents, there was no such protection for those who loved, looked after, and then had to leave theirs behind.

Our small son Mark took to his new keeper immediately. She had put on a royal blue overall as soon as she had unpacked and after a cursory inspection of the nursery asked us to get her a fender for the large open nursery fire. "I'd like a large cage-like variety and then I can air the nappies on it." The disposable variety had yet to become commonplace.

We, the Hall family, embarked on an era that was to last for 43 years. Inevitably Mark was called James for several weeks, but who was he to complain? He had someone who played and laughed and cuddled and took him out on the back of her bike to feed the ducks at Rockland Staithe. Her favourite expression, which punctuated most sentences, was 'sort of thing.' As is so often the case, we all started saying it. She liked "ordinary food, sort of thing" which meant "nothing fancy, sort of thing" and was clearly no gourmet, often preferring a marmite sandwich by the fire in the nursery to the supper that I proffered. Any small child who attempted to evade bedtime by hiding behind the sofa, or anywhere else for that matter, was merely 'prolonging time and such like' another endearing nannyism which we all took to.

It was everyone's delight when my daughter Alice was born at home, and for the months that I breastfed her, Nanny and I shared her care. Unlike those horror tales of nannies who resented anyone 'interfering' in the upbringing of 'their' children, I never resisted the temptation of picking up my baby whenever I felt like it even if Nanny had only just got her settled. After all, I was only 25 and I too adored babies. The smell of Johnson's' baby powder seemed to permeate the house, festoons of washing were draped daily on the line, and the nursery was the centre of the house.

In those days we adhered to the four hourly feed routine rather than the demand feeding of today. After a lusty slurp and the expulsion of the supposed 'wind' Alice would be tucked firmly up in her cradle at night, or the pram during the day, parked under a tree outside, regardless of the weather with, if necessary, the hood and canopy for cover. If the wind blew then the pram rocked. Alice could see the leaves in the tree above her and hear the birds. The only concession was a net, which covered the pram to deter any visiting cats from sharing her refuge. Try that on modern mothers of today who seem to have no respite either day or night from their babies, permanently welded to their sides, or crawling round their feet, 'demanding' being the operative word from birth.

Very soon I, who knew little about babies, was learning all I needed to know from someone who, in my eyes, knew it all. Bath time soon after six o'clock, story time and bedtime were non negotiable and consequently never an issue. Routine was the order of the nursery day which I soon realised suited us all. The horrors of today's baby alarms which summon parents to pick up their offspring at the onset of the slightest sleepy grizzle, and even worse, bring them downstairs as if to entertain any assembled supper guests would not have been to Nanny's liking. Nor was it or is it to mine.

Unlike me, she never seemed to be tired or cross. If one could make graphs of human temperaments, hers would chart an even line, seldom going up or down and certainly never rising or falling dramatically. I found that extraordinary. Being the antithesis of that and prone to hyperbole and exaggeration, I would enthuse wildly about something which she would merely describe as 'quite nice.' With the arrival of Jeremy in 1964 our family was complete and Nanny, far from feeling overburdened, was jubilant. Born at home and weighing 10 pounds, the new baby soon became the proverbial pet, the more so as with his easygoing temperament Nanny was able to boast that "he's never given a minute's trouble, this one".

Those were the days before mothers' helps and foreign au pairs outnumbered old-fashioned nannies. And those were the days when nursery tea was just that, with "bread and butter first dare" with lashings of chocolate spread or treacle as acceptable wickedness.

Although they were never malicious, there was nonetheless a certain rivalry between nannies of that era and a distinct pecking order. Reassuring as it was to know that ours batted for the home side, such remarks as "I told Nanny Knollys that Clarinda needed bigger shoes" inevitably caused a blush or two. Nanny Hall was certainly direct and became more so as she got older. Mercifully she had a splendid sense of humour and took teasing in her stride. How else would she have survived six years in the WAAF? Any crisis or catastrophe was explained away as 'just one of those things', an expression that this matter of fact lady applied to whatever occasion merited it.

Milk of Magnesia or Syrup of Figs was then what Calpol is today – the remedy for everything from teething problems to temper tantrums. Hidden in a drawer was Ex-lax. This potent laxative, which looked and tasted like chocolate held special appeal for Alice who, after surreptitiously locating it, swallowed all that remained in the packet and suffered horribly. Nanny, ever solicitous, far from being cross and certainly not panicked, merely remarked, "Well, dare, I don't expect you'll do that again will you?" She did not, but what she did do was to indulge her passion for sweets by other means. At Claxton primary school pupils were encouraged to buy a savings stamp each week with a picture of Princess Anne on it, and to stick it into a special savings book. At the end of term, Mark's book was returned full and Alice's empty. So what had happened to the supposed contributions? They had been spent in the shop next door to the school. Not on stamps of course, but sweets.

We young mums lucky enough to have one, learned from our nannies. Our children were, I suppose, in the safe care of professionals whose patience was limitless, who provided continuity and security, yet who enjoyed life with children and who were, above all, fun. Unlike the days when the nursery and the rest of the house were virtually segregated and children saw little of their parents, we seemed to have the best of both worlds. We had the freedom to go out without having to import babysitters. I was able to pursue my very part-time and somewhat amateurish career in television, and yet when we wanted to extricate the children from their nursery routine, we did so without any resultant long faces.

But this story is about Nanny, not her charges or her employers, although inevitably they featured prominently throughout her life. Her day off was Wednesday and it usually followed the same pattern. Clad in trousers and boots she would appear from the garage with her moped. Out came the spanner so that the sparking plug from the Lambretta could be put under the grill in the kitchen to dry out, before being given a quick clean with a nail file. This routine evidently ensured that the kick-start would be effective sooner than later. It would be ten o'clock before she donned the crash lid, put Jeremy on the seat and pushed him down the drive before waving goodbye to him, and phut phutting down the road to Norwich, and thence to

Station Road, Snettisham. There she would spend the day with her nonagenarian Aunt Lizzie, the sister of her mother, always referred to as Mrs Bales. The journey itself would probably take nearly two hours, and on arrival Nanny would be required to deal with any jobs that the old lady couldn't cope with herself. Hedge cutting seemed to feature frequently, as did tidying up the front and back gardens. The cottage itself sounded primitive but was nothing unusual to Nanny. Her father, who was a retired gardener, and her mother, who had been in domestic service, were strict, god-fearing, elderly parents, albeit kind and loving. The cottage in which they all lived in Heacham was a humble carrstone dwelling of the two up and two down variety, with a front room that was seldom used. Anyone taken short in the dark would have to carry a candle down to the bottom of the back garden. Invariably it blew out leaving its bearer in the dark.

With both her parents now dead, Nanny talked frequently about her family and in particular her sister Ada who was 13 years older than her, now living in Peterborough with her husband Cecil Flint. Their children, Nanny's 'neffoo' and niece Tony and Joan and their families, featured regularly in conversations as well as in visits, and I never queried that her family was anything unusual.

Sundays during her childhood in Heacham consisted of church in the morning and chapel in the afternoon, one parent being Church of England and the other Methodist. Strict disciplinarians whose mantra was to 'make do and mend', they could neither afford nor tolerate frills, so life was austere but happy. No cooking or activity of any kind was allowed on the Sabbath unless it was of a religious nature. Sunday lunch was cooked on Saturday and eaten cold the next day. When funds were low it was 'bread and pullit' which for years I mistakenly interpreted as bread and chicken. Reading was permitted but only religious books or the Bible. Nanny had one present on her birthday and one at Christmas, both of them books which were read and re-read. I have one of them still. Carefully covered in brown paper, with all the illustrations crayoned in, it was clearly one of her prized possession, all of which had to be taken care of. Frugality was ingrained in her and yet her generosity knew no bounds. Each Christmas Eve Nanny would appear laden with items for the children's stockings which she had collected during the year.

The strange thing was that she had no regard for possessions, and was therefore always difficult to please as far as presents were concerned. Ornaments she would deem 'dust traps', she never used any sort of cosmetics and clothes would be gratefully received but seldom worn, and certainly not for months if not years. From teenage days she had made her own and then mended them, knitted her own jerseys and then unpicked them, washed the wool and reknitted it in a different pattern.

Looking back on those early days when she first came to us, it must have been something of a disappointment for her to find that I too was a dressmaker and made and smocked nearly all my children's' clothes. But knitting bored me and she churned out wonderful ribbed and Fairisle patterned jerseys, as well as finishing half constructed garments on which I had embarked and then abandoned. Only when she said, "I suppose that will be another jersey that I shall have to finish", was I spurred into completing three Arran jerseys (in quick knit wool of course, large needles) for all the children. That Mark spilled Copydex down the front of his remains a painful memory, the more so as he also hid it under the sofa where it remained for days – too late to remedy the congealed and rubberised front.

Nanny and Mrs Lawrence

We also had an elderly village lady, Mrs Lawrence, who came in to clean two mornings a week. The relationship was amicable – just, but there was definitely rivalry. After her day off, great was Nanny's delight at saying, "I see Mrs Lawrence has been at the washing again. The woollies are all matted". Indeed I had also been vexed to find a particularly nice new jersey of mine reduced to a doll's dimensions after she had decided to boil it. Explaining that that was what she always did with things that had stains, she didn't think it was worth taking home and boiling in her copper, so she had done it in my jam saucepan. Worse would be Nanny's, 'hmm, funny that everything's pink. I daresay Mrs Lawrence put that red shirt in with the whites'.

When a new washing machine was installed there was triumph in the air. "I don't suppose Mrs Lawrence will be able to work that". Dead right. She couldn't. When I offered her our old one she accepted it and subsequently described it as 'alright' when questioned as to its use. Maybe it just stood in her outhouse as an ornament. I never saw or heard it working when I visited her cottage. Nor could she work, let alone empty, the vacuum cleaner, answer the telephone, deal with any of 'them new gadgety things', but oh boy, could she scrub. Would that we had more floors that needed such treatment rather than the meagre areas of the scullery and tack-room whose tiles were scrubbed whether or not they needed it. With her hair in a tight bun, her expansive figure with its large low-slung bosom in a wraparound floral overall, and her ill fitting false teeth, in only 'when there's company' she had brought up 5 children of her own as well as an indeterminate number of grandchildren. The primitive farm workers' cottage in which the family lived smelt of a mixture of cats, wet knickers and carbolic soap. When she and her husband Snap were eventually rehoused by the council she told me that she didn't think that their 'sexual shed' was going to fit in the new garden. I still think fondly of Mrs Lawrence whenever the word 'sectional' prefaces a building. When I asked her if our horsebox could help in the move she replied, "Well, I'll ha' te get in connection wi' him about that". But possibly the most memorable piece of information divulged was when, at the height of the troubles in Northern Ireland, she told me Snap had to go to see the specialist 'up Norwich' because 'the doctor reckon he got ulsters in his back passage'. Rather meanly I made her say it twice.

I never saw Snap without his hat, even when I visited him in his cottage. Nor did I see him without the stub of a cigarette protruding from his yellowing moustache. He wore thick breeches throughout the year, old leather buskins and boots of a bygone era, and the timing of his twice-daily ambles down to the allotment where he kept his pigs were timed like clockwork. He had retired after a lifetime working on the land and, if ever there was a true countryman, he was one. His stock reply to my enquiries about his health, his pigs, his hens, and his vegetable garden never varied. They were always 'fairly.'

Chapter 2

Inevitably, there were irritations. That Nanny always beat Tom, the most tolerant of men, to the kettle before breakfast, announcing daily that "the kettle HAS boiled" exasperated him and became something of a family joke. Not so funny was the fact that she had no sense of smell and could be guaranteed to leave black smoke belching from saucepans or toasters that I had inadvertently left unattended. But only once did we have a major set to.

Hugely pregnant and within days of giving birth to Jeremy at home, I was more than tetchy to discover that to get to our bathroom I had to negotiate an obstacle course of pillows, blankets and the entire contents of the airing cupboard. "What on earth are you doing?", I snapped. "Well, it needed a good clear out and better before the baby than afterwards", she replied. She had a point which enraged me further.

Tom, originally a qualified mechanical engineer, ran a Norfolk Broads boatyard which, with three friends and co-directors, we had collectively bought. The Beaver Fleet at St Olaves on the River Waveney consisted of hire cruisers, built and let to holidaymakers throughout the summer season, and enjoyed by us from time to time. But boats held no appeal for Nanny. She 'did not like the water' and although she could swim, just, she seldom did. Nor did she relish the increasing passion for ponies that was rapidly consuming Alice. Charlie, a supposedly docile first pony soon turned out to be a recalcitrant fiend in the stable with an inclination to bite, kick or both. He met his demise one night after a violent attack of colic that may have been our good fortune, except that we had a small inconsolable daughter to deal with. But children recover quickly from disasters such as death, and transfer their affections with alarming rapidity. Unlike the budgerigar that had a Christian burial under the fig tree, Charlie was winched up into the trailer of the local hunt in the middle of the night, and therefore disappeared before Alice was up. She was less distressed when the hamster disappeared down the entrance to the ventilation tunnel running under the house to the drawing room fireplace. It was never seen again, but at least as it was summer time there was no fire in the grate. It was of course 'just one of those things.' The children's main concern was that there was no body to bury. When our shaggy ginger cat disappeared it might be assumed that our animal husbandry left much to be desired. It improved over the years and the only further fatalities were caused by canine old age.

Jeremy, Mark and Alice on Ginny

Ginny was soon installed as Charlie's replacement, and as she could be driven as well as ridden soon gained Nanny's approval. Up we would all get into the governess cart and head off down the village with a picnic tea. It took me an indeterminate length of time to catch the pony in the field, despite the fact that she wore a head collar with a string attached, so my enthusiasm was somewhat blunted. Round and round we would go until Ginny succumbed to my pleas, not to mention bribes of oats, to be caught. Her eventual capture would then be followed by my having either to wash or brush off the mud with which she had caked herself whilst rolling – yet another perverse trick to thwart my efforts to get her harnessed and into the trap. The resultant pleasure was, I suppose, worth all the effort, and nanny's picnic teas were my reward.

Next came Gypsy – fat, obliging if and when she felt like it, and distinctly benign. She even took no exception to being cast in the circus pony role when Alice leapt from the stable rafters on to her very wide back, or more usually onto her own bottom on the straw floor. Nanny, though prepared to proffer an occasional titbit from over the stable door, had no inclination to enter therein. Little did either of us

Alice on Gypsy

know that we were in for years of horse activities when both Mark and Alice graduated from the Pony Club to the eventing scene, and instead of heading for the local hunter trials it was the Badminton and Burghley three day events that were in their sights.

Luckily for Nanny, Jeremy showed no inclination to ride, preferring instead to sit in the seat on the back of Nanny's pushbike, while she did the pedalling to and from Rockland Staithe. There a loaf of bread was dispensed to the very fat resident ducks, so that they became even fatter. Alternatively, he'd play in the pit he had dug in our copse, or indulge in endless mock battles with his friend Chrissy Knollys, born within 3 days of him. Soldiers would be laid out amongst the logs under the stairs and the manoeuvres were conducted in apparent silence. If time to go home arrived before the defeated army was packed away, then placements remained to be continued at a later date. If the log basket needed filling, tough.

When we suggested that Nanny might come with us when we went skiing, the predictable answer was forthcoming. "Good gracious me no. All that snow". Nor did she fancy our camping forays to Cornwall with caravan, boat, tents and a few extra children. As it usually rained relentlessly from our arrival to our departure, she had a point.

Until Jeremy was old enough to come too, Nanny stayed happily behind with him, minding the house, the labrador, the bantams, and any hamster, gerbil, budgerigar that might have been in residence. Ponies remained safely in the field. Trips by bus to Norwich to visit the museum were a highlight, as were excursions on the train to

Nanny and Jeremy (1965)

Yarmouth. We always knew that with Nanny at home, all would be well. It always was. When Jeremy was old enough to come skiing too, we wondered if it came up to those happy times. When Nanny herself was away, far from feeling any pleasure in having the house to ourselves, we all missed her. She had that rare gift of being able to live with a family without ever being intrusive. Just as Mrs Ashworth had foretold, she still liked 'to keep herself to herself', and in the evenings, when the children were in bed and the toys put away, the nursery was her territory despite the array of garments airing on the fender round the log fire – just as she had requested.

Her sense of fun and her laughter were never far from the surface. From being an obliging pack animal crawling across the nursery floor laden with children, to whizzing down the tarzan tree slide or running races in the garden, she was always game. She even tolerated unmerciful teasing when she enrolled for French lessons from a village elder who could probably speak, but certainly couldn't teach the language. Why would Nanny want to say 'l'ascenseur ne marche pas.' We didn't have a lift, and certainly not one that was broken. Her aptitude or lack of it for a foreign language can't have helped, and the sentences that we practised at meal times diminished as rapidly as her attendance at classes.

"I don't think I'm cut out for speaking French, sort of thing", she said sagely. "Non, Nanny, non" we agreed.

Another steep learning curve bit the dust after we tried driving lessons. There was clearly going to be difficulty passing the test, caused by a seeming inability ever to look in the rear mirror. Instead, she'd turn full circle in the driving seat to look through the rear window to see that nothing was coming before careering in fast jerks, jumping forward and off. Many a time I took over when my nerves were in tatters and she'd say, "I think I'm better when there isn't any traffic around". But she suddenly hit upon the idea that if she had a three-wheeler Reliant Robin car her motorbike licence would be sufficient.

As soon as said done and off she went on a trawl of garages in search of one. The Lambretta soon fell from favour with the arrival of what we labelled The Red Peril. It was short lived and came to grief when it failed to negotiate a sharp bend at Claxton and climbed a bank instead. Nanny, who stepped out unscathed concluded that, as was the case with French, "I don't think I'm cut out for driving sort of thing. Strange really because when I was a WAAF I used to do engine tests in the workshop". The moped and the pushbike were back in favour to our great relief.

We were a good team, Nanny and I. She hated cooking. I enjoyed it. Pulverised vegetables, glutinous gravy and lumpy chocolate semolina were her specialities – the latter always greatly enjoyed by the children. But she delighted in the day to day domesticity of clearing up the kitchen, tidying the house (always necessary) or ironing piles of garments, all of which I abhorred, preferring to labour in the garden or the stables as well as pursuing my career in television.

On Mondays and Thursdays I headed for London by train, and then to Lime Grove to present the BBC current affairs programme Nationwide, or to go out with a camera crew and director to film various stories. For the years prior to that I had been on the rota of presenters for the local programme Look East as well as having a weekly cooking spot for which a mini kitchen had been set up in the studio. Fine until the arrival of Jeremy was imminent, and I was growing larger by the week. It had to come to a halt. The producer thought otherwise and with the ingenuity of the floor manager prolonged my tenure for several weeks by putting blocks under the table legs behind which I stood to do my demos. My bump may have been suitably hidden from the viewers, but stirring and sloshing ingredients on a surface one could barely reach across was far from ideal. I remember asking Nanny what she thought of one particular item which had gone disastrously wrong, when a bowl full of beaten egg skidded across the floor straight at a camera. She had replied dismissively, "Oh, I don't watch. I see you trying things out in the kitchen here, and anyway, you're on at bath time". Just one of those things. Inevitably the time came for me to quit and a new face was introduced to the Look East kitchen. It was Delia Smith. I've been a devotee of hers ever since and her books have been and still are my favourite cookery tomes. Years later when I met her at a dinner in London I reminded her that her launch on Look East shot her into culinary orbit which it had certainly never done for me.

Three years later I returned to the BBC, not to cook but to rejoin the rota of presenters for Look East and it was from there that I was recruited for Nationwide. This was a national rather than a regional programme with far greater resources, and more demanding professionally. Whereas I had been familiar with working the old fashioned Autocue pedal as one would a sewing machine, and reading off it according to the speed I treddled, suddenly I was in front of three cameras instead of one, with a special operator working my Autocue. It was television luxury.

I look back with gratitude and amazement at the indulgence of my respective bosses. Remaining freelance, I had an annual contract that gave me the freedom to work a mere two days a week during the school term times rather than the holidays, and the option to opt out of dates that I couldn't manage – unheard of today. Michael Bunce, the programme editor, greeted me on one occasion with, "Hallo Susanne, good of you to spare the time!" When I asked him why he indulged me thus his reply was honest. "Well, you're representative of a chunk of our viewers. You're a housewife with children at school, and you live in the country". No reference to the fact that I had the privilege of employing a Nanny to hold the fort at home, which could hardly be described as representative. "And you counterbalance Sue Lawley's glamour and professionalism. Michael Barratt gives us the hard journalism and Bobo (Bob Wellings) the softer balances". It has to be said that I was less than happy to be cast in the pinafored plain Jane role. Luckily, Sue Lawley, far from being a rival, was and remains a good friend and yes she was, and still is, both glamorous and very professional.

The era of 'celebs' was a mere speck in the future. We were never paid the extortionate sums that presenters today seem able to command, but we were nonetheless generously rewarded. My earnings put the icing on the family cake, made sure that Nanny's original £3.10 shillings a week was upped, as well as eventually helping to finance a swimming pool.

At home my appearance on the nursery television would prompt a quick switch of channels. No one wanted to watch Mum until a possible financial aspect was spotted. Mark showed an early aptitude for entrepreneurial skills when enquiring whether he could sell my autographs, and if so for how much? The fact that I interviewed famous people from time to time was only of interest if I returned with autographs, preferably of pop stars or sportsmen. Pete Townsend of The Who was deemed a worthwhile trophy but David Niven, Gregory Peck, Cary Grant or Omar Sharif – who were they?

Nanny with Alice and Jeremy (1968)

The real hit of the small screen was Blue Peter, which was seldom missed. After Nanny or I had fetched the children from Claxton Primary School, tea and then their favourite programme followed. There was their heroine Val Singleton telling children how to make dog kennels out of empty cornflakes packets, and Santa Claus out of an empty Fairy liquid bottle, little realising that if the receptacles were not ALREADY empty, they soon would be. Alice in particular showed no scruples in pouring cereal into the bin in order to procure the packet. When Val Singleton joined Nationwide and actually came to stay with us in Norfolk, heaven was near. Nanny remained unphased, remarking only that "she looks better in real life, doesn't she?" She said the same of Sue Lawley.

It wasn't just our children who benefited from the aura of continuity and security engendered by Nanny. Their parents did too. Things that might have seemed frightening to both of us such as a nasty version of measles or earache were all commonplace to her.

She'd seen it all before. On discovering that we had an embryonic pyromaniac in the family, she was unphased. The evidence was plain for all to see – a burnt out waste paper basket in Nanny's bedroom was not a case of self-ignition. It was the result of one small boy with a fascination for matches, who thought it might be exciting to see what happened if he set fire to the old newspapers in the said waste paper basket. He was suitably chastened, as well as frightened by the experience. Nanny, having smothered the fire with the help of a blanket remarked, "I don't think Mark will be quite so keen on setting fire to things after that, do you?"

Her capacity to remain impervious to almost anything that happened was one of her most endearing qualities. Her, 'well, it's just one of those things' fitted every eventuality and whatever I deemed a crisis or disaster she reduced to a mere inconvenience. Equally, triumphs were low on the Richter scale. When as a teenager Alice was chosen to ride in the Junior British Event team for the European Championships to be held at Burghley, she merely remarked, "Well that'll be quite nice, won't it? But while I think of it I'll be needing some more name tapes for Jeremy".

That she was ever at ease and able to befriend children so easily was in stark contrast to her seeming reluctance to make friends for herself. She saw and enjoyed the company of other Nannies yet never progressed beyond acquaintanceship, even though Nanny Colman (Miss Goose) and she would meet occasionally in Norwich on days out. I never understood the reasons for her seeming inability to make friends, particularly as there were rare occasions when she could be so gregarious. Mrs Ashworth had spotted it years ago and her prophesy that Nanny would probably always 'keep herself to herself' was to cost her dear in old age when her memory failed and loneliness stalked.

Chapter 3

By the time all three children were at school, Nanny embarked on her secondary career, taking care of such chores as mending and what she called 'sides-to-middling' of worn sheets, as well as brass and silver cleaning. "Well, you see, when I was in service with the Master of Caius College in Cambridge, we used to help the butler do that". Even better was the fact that the same butler had taught her to carve. I never tired of hearing about her days behind the green baize door, of the fun that she had in the servant's hall, and her acceptance of domestic life as it was before World War II. But it was to be many years before the jig saw puzzle and the flip side of her life were revealed.

When Jeremy went away to boarding school and we no longer had need of a Nanny, there was no way that we could part with her or she

5 School Lane, Rockland St Mary

with us. We bought her a small cottage in the village so that she would always have the security of a home of her own. The freehold was to be hers and Number 5 School Lane was duly put into her name. She had asked if instead of being our living-in Nanny she could remain with us on a daily basis, to clean and mind the house. If we were away she would come and live in. There was no need for us to mull that over. It would ensure that Nanny would remain part of our family for the foreseeable future. Twiglets and banana sandwiches were still served at teatime during the school holidays, but in the living room of School Lane rather than the nursery of the Old Hall. Years later it became the secret rendezvous for Nanny and our children's planning of a surprise silver wedding party for Tom and me. Both the grandmothers were hidden there until it was time for our unexpected guests to suddenly make an appearance while we were at some friends' house in the next-door village, lured there on some pretext which all those in the know had carefully choreographed. We returned to find the paddock filled with cars and a wonderful collection of friends and relations to greet us. Nanny was not just good at children's parties.

The Lambretta now a thing of the past, Nanny came to work each day on her bicycle, and caught the bus on her days or weekends out. As her aunt Mrs Bales had died aged 106, she had no further need to go to Snettisham, so instead would visit her sister Ada in Peterborough. At home in Rockland she continued to 'keep herself to herself' rather than make new friends in the village, relying instead on two of long standing. Mrs Steward, whose Christian name was evidently not used (and who called Nanny Miss Church rather than Mary) was housekeeper to a widower living in Stibbard. During her time there with the Ashworths, Nanny and she had got to know each other and often met up in Norwich on days off. Describing her somewhat deprecatingly as 'rather dull' they nevertheless went on holiday together. Great was our amusement to get a postcard telling us that they had been to the cinema in Eastbourne but the film was so sexy that Mrs Steward's hat had fallen off. The other friend was a lifelong one, Mrs Stannard, formerly Florrie Williamson. She and Nanny had grown up together in Heacham, and had kept in touch with each other ever since.

The Lapsley family also remained close. Squadron Leader John Lapsley, a Battle of Britain fighter pilot, and his wife Jean asked WAAF Mary Church if she would consider looking after their two small children after she was demobbed. This she readily agreed to do, and five very happy years followed the war when she, as well as Jean, were back in civvy street. Air Marshal Sir John and Lady Lapsley, as they became, and Penny and Peter their children, who I shall write about later, never failed to remember their Nanny, of whom they had become and remained so fond. Cards and presents (invariably edible) at Christmas and on her birthday gave enormous pleasure, and their visits to Rockland were red-letter days. As Nanny's birthday on October 30th 1983 approached, Tom and I asked her, as we did each year, what treat she would like? "I'd quite like to go to Thursford to see the Mighty Wurlitzer". This was a museum that housed some magnificent old organs, which used to accompany the silent movies. It

Peter and Penny Lapsey (1952)

was a request that was easy enough to fulfil. But this would be her 70th birthday, and therefore it needed to be extra special. Thus all three children were told that no matter what they were doing, their presence was required. Tom happily agreed to take a day off from work and booked us all a table for lunch in the hotel by the river at Wroxham. Everyone duly assembled, and together with our Labrador Jess we piled into the car for our day's outing. After lunch, we walked along the riverbank before visiting Thursford to marvel at all the exhibits, and to listen to the playing of the famous machine. As we finally made our way home somewhat wearily, Nanny remarked that she had had a lovely day thank you. It had really been 'quite nice.' Praise indeed.

"Well, Nanny, it's not every day that you have a birthday and certainly not a seventieth".

"No" she said "that'll be the day. Only one more year to go. I shall be 70 next year, as you know".

No one said a word as all eyes turned towards me. Hadn't I insisted that everyone must make the extra effort to honour the special birthday of a special member of our family? Had I got them all there under false pretences, and were they all going to have to repeat the whole exercise the following year? Yes, and yes. Mum had made a complete cock-up for want of a more explicit description, and although she would not be challenged in front of Nanny, she could expect (and got) a roasting in the privacy of home.

How on earth had I got it so wrong? After the initial universal rage, humour crept in and we have probably laughed more about Nanny's phantom 70th than we have about any of my other gaffes.

Although as the so-called local television personality I was frequently asked to open fetes or cut ribbons, I was ill prepared to deal with an invitation to join the Mothers Union. As the wife of a churchwarden, surely I would do so? No, I would not, but what about Nanny? A regular churchgoer all her life as well as the quintessential mother figure, she would make a splendid member and might even make some new friends. Good idea. But the enrolling member looked aghast.

"She's not a mother", she spluttered.

"Well, perhaps not, but she's been mother to more children than you and I put together", was my instant reply. Nanny joined, attended, and enjoyed the meetings, though she did remark that the organiser was "a very bossy lady.".

"More so than me?"

"Oh no, I wouldn't say that". The lady was nothing if not direct.

"And they keep asking me questions about all of us. Of course I don't say anything. What business is it of theirs?" Such was her loyalty to us that on one occasion when we were away on holiday one of our friends telephoned to ask when we would be back. She told me later that the answer had been, "I'll tell them that you rang when they return". Thus we knew that just as she 'kept herself to herself' so she guarded our privacy too.

The WI she would have none of. There was a lively and active branch in the village but any suggestion that she should join was met with a firm shake of the head, the mouth pursed and a "No, that's not for me. All that jam making and such like. And all that gossiping". Instead she bought a knitting machine and it was mooted that perhaps the nursery might soon be a woollies workroom. It was not to be. So complicated were the instructions that after hours of toil, when all of us tried in vain to get it set up, Nanny remarked "I never had all this trouble when I put a Bedford truck engine together when I was in the WAAF". One or two garments were eventually constructed, but it was not long before the knitting needles were out again and the machine back in its cardboard box under her bed at School Lane. There it remained until, with the sewing machine, it eventually went the way of so many things – into the house clearance van twenty years later.

Chapter 4

By 1989 I had been a widow for five years. I was still living at Rockland, but alone. Both our sons were away working in London, our daughter was married with a baby, also living in London but looking for a house in Norfolk. I knew that they were right when they said I really should move. I had first realised this to be true after the terrifying gales on the night of October 11th 1987 when a 20' Jacobean chimney had crashed down through the spare bedroom into the dining room below. I was on the other side of the wall and when I staggered to the door in the dark (no lights were working) only to find that it wouldn't open, I grabbed my duvet and headed through the other door which led through another room to the landing. I all but choked on the dust which greeted me, so quickly fled into the garden until daybreak. The telephone lines were down, punctured pipes spurted water, a fallen tree blocked the drive, and there was chaos everywhere around me. First Nanny joined me, unruffled as ever and

Old Hall, Rockland St Mary (before 11.10.87)

Old Hall after 11.10.87
Chimney and pigeon loft gone.

merely remarking that the duvet would need washing. Then my ever-solicitous neighbours, David and Dawn Scott, came to my rescue, followed by my sons who had to take a circuitous and lengthy route from London in order to avoid fallen trees. The insurance company, inundated with claims from anguished householders, eventually financed a massive repair job, which took a year and cost thousands. When the house was at last in comparatively good order, a developer made a large offer to buy me out. But where would I go, and what about Nanny? Well, I'd think about that when I needed to but until I had somewhere to move to there was little urgency. It had been a roller coaster five years for me, trying to overcome the loss of my husband whilst at the same time keeping a semblance of normality for the homecomings of my children and their friends, as well as resuming my television work which had encompassed the making of various documentaries.

I embarked on a half-hearted attempt to look for another house, but as I didn't know what I wanted or where to look it was a rather feeble effort. Rockland had been home for 28 years and remained my refuge. Anyone who has suffered the trauma of the death of a spouse, as I had, will know that one clings to home and memories in the wreckage rather than face a strange new world. Familiarity becomes doubly precious and the prospect of losing it, frightening. I had been a teenage bride and practical and resourceful as I had become over the years, I had no concept of the single life in adulthood. Nanny became my lifeline, unflappable, calm as ever. She had a tranquillity about her that was balm. Nothing, but nothing ever seemed to rattle her. Equally, she never seemed to get excited. Life in its entirety was 'just one of those things.' That she was always 'there' for me gave huge comfort rather than what she said, which was very little. She was not emotional by nature and certainly not demonstrative. But she was always the same and helped me so much in my feeble attempts to carry on as before, when the future seemed so daunting. When I was apologetic after one of my frequent tearful interludes, that wonderful phrase, 'It's just one of those things', would be my comfort.

Aged 75, she still came to work on her bicycle, the brass and silver still sparkled, the kettle HAD boiled and life went on. She was by then a veteran member of the Mothers' Union and as such one of those privileged to be transported to meetings by the Vicar, Kit Chalcraft, in his yellow minibus.

What I hadn't bargained for was someone else finding me a suitable house, let alone my daughter Alice. Having decided to move out of London, she and her husband Christopher spent any spare weekend searching Norfolk for a new venue for their furniture making business, as well as a house in which to live. While I looked after their baby, Thomas, they scoured the county estate agents as well as any suitable premises. But far from finding what they wanted, they just happened to see the very house for me when they were in Swaffham. Georgian, shabby, with a large garden, all of it in need of modernisation and therefore reasonably priced, it sounded just the thing and a project to boot. Suddenly, it was not a question of leaving Rockland which I had so dreaded, but rather of going to Swaffham which was exciting. But what about Nanny? We all agreed that leaving her would be out of the question, but what if she chose to stay? I'd better ask her. Would she like to sell her cottage and buy another near us? Her answer astonished me.

"Well, yes, I would but only when I've made a will so that I can leave it to you".

"Good gracious me, no", I retorted somewhat astonished. "You must definitely make a will, but you must leave it to your family".

"That's just it", she said. "You're my family now. I never had a real one of my own. You see I was a foundling and my name is not really Mary Church. I've wanted to tell you for years and years, but I've never been able to talk about it".

I had never seen her look so distressed. Had she not been tee-total all her life, I would probably have poured us both a stiff drink.

"I was abandoned by my mother at St Mary-le-Strand Church in London. That's how I got my name. It was on December 13th 1914, so I like to think that perhaps it was not that she didn't want me but perhaps my father had been killed in the war and she couldn't afford to keep me, especially if she already had some other children. I was apparently about 2 months old. I was taken to a Dr Barnardo's home and I stayed there until I was three. That's why I always wanted to look after children, and that's why I could never marry because I didn't have a proper birth certificate. You see I didn't know if I was illegitimate. When I was young that was very shameful. And even now, after all these years, I still can't talk about it. And I've never told any of the people that I've worked for".

"Didn't the Lapsleys know?" I asked.

"Oh, good gracious me, no. I've never wanted anyone to know, and anyway, I've never been able to talk about it".

And she never could until the day she died, even though I gradually and very carefully managed to extract the odd nugget from time to time without distressing her. Such had been the stigma that she had felt was attached to her, that it had, quite literally, affected her whole life.

By this time tears were coursing down Nanny's cheeks, and mine too. Telling her that I thought hers was a most remarkable story and that she was even more special than I had always thought had no effect. "In fact you're just as special as Moses in the bulrushes" I tried. That at least coaxed a smile.

"Nanny, you must tell me all about your early life because it's absolutely fascinating, not just to me but to lots of other people too. I'd like to write about you. It's social history".

"Oh no!" Evident horror at the thought. A lifetime of secrecy could not possibly be divulged in her lifetime. "Not until I'm gone. When that time comes it'll all be over and then of course you can write about me. But I can't imagine that anyone would be interested in all that sort of thing. Tony and Betty my niece and nephoo have often been on about it, but I just say to them that I don't want to talk about it and whatever interest is it to them?"

"OK Nanny. I accept that, but one day maybe…"

I tried skirting round the subject on many occasions hoping to glean more information, but little was ever forthcoming beyond her duties as a housemaid and then as a Nanny, and on each occasion she became withdrawn and all but tearful. Strange really that it was the prospect of either or both of us moving house that had unlocked a story that dumbfounded me then, and still does today.

Chapter 5

Heacham, a large village on the North Norfolk coast overlooking the Wash, is a popular holiday resort, where hundreds of mobile homes and caravans are parked near the beach to cater for the influx of thousands of tourists in the summer months. The large Norman church stands on a hill surrounded by prosperous looking traditional carrstone houses as well as modern buildings. It was not so at the end of the 19th and beginning of the 20th centuries. Then it was a small close-knit community where everyone knew each other as well as where they lived, with most families being dependent on the land for a living. Boys grew up expecting to become farm workers and girls to go into domestic service with the many so-called gentlefolk that lived in the larger houses. These included the three elderly Miss Black sisters who would play such a critical role in the life of Mary Church.

The coming of the railway in 1862 had heralded a new era for the village, making it possible for townspeople from King's Lynn to come by train, to walk down to the miles of sandy beach and enjoy a day at the seaside, or even in one of the wooden beach huts that had sprung up along the coast.

There was also Pocahontas, the 17th century exotic Red Indian princess from Virginia who married John Rolfe, the son of the Lord of the Manor of Heacham Hall, who gradually became a great tourist draw. One cannot but wonder if the bitter winds of Norfolk might have contributed to her early death at the age of 22 just as she was about to embark from Gravesend for a journey home to America. Hers was a short life but a far-reaching one nonetheless.

Thanks to the well researched work of historians, the tale of Captain John Smith who took an expedition of three ships and 105 men to the new world in 1606 is well chronicled. They sailed into Chesapeake Bay in 1607, and thence up a river, which they named James, to a peninsular where they could moor close to the shore. Here they established a colony which became and remains Jamestown. As might be expected, the lure to explore further inland prevailed and as

St Mary the Virgin, Heacham

The memorial to Pocahontas above that to her husband John Rolfe reads:

PRINCESS
MATOAKA REBECKA POCAHONTAS
DAUGHTER OF POWHATAN HEREDITARY OVERKING
OF THE ALGONQUIN INDIANS OF VIRGINIA
BORN 1595 BAPTISED 1613 DIED 1617
HER ROMANTIC MARRIAGE IN 1614 TO
JOHN ROLFE
BROUGHT PEACE TO THE SETTLEMENT
TO MARK A PICTURESQUE EPISODE
IN THE HISTORY OF TWO NATIONS
THIS MEMORIAL WAS SET UP
BY FRIENDS IN
ENGLAND AND AMERICA
1933

Village sign showing Pocahontas

relations with the local Indians seemed cordial, the risks were deemed minimal. But it was not long before things soured and Captain Smith was captured and taken to the Great Chief Powhatan, who decided that he should be killed. This was far from the liking of his 12-year-old daughter, the Princess Pocahontas, who interceded, pleading for mercy to be shown and thus saving his life. In the ensuing years she came often to Jamestown bearing gifts of food and fruit for the settlers. In 1612 other settlers arrived and knowing that the Indians held some Englishmen prisoner, they lured Pocahontas on board one of their ships as a hostage with which to barter for their release. She was taken to Jamestown and lived in the house of Reverend Alexander Whitaker where she was instructed in the Christian faith and later baptised – the first Indian to take such a step. Whilst there she met a young widower John Rolfe of Heacham whose bride she later became, with the blessing of her father Great Chief Powhatan. Their son, Thomas, was born in Virginia in 1615, before they returned to England with the Governor Sir Thomas Dale and a retinue of attendants. Pocahontas, now known as Lady Rebecka, became the centre of attention at banquets and receptions and was received at the court of King James I by his consort Queen Anne.

When the Rolfes visited John's mother at Heacham Hall, legend has it that they planted a mulberry tree in the garden. Since then hundreds, if not thousands of Americans, claiming direct descent from the Indian Princess, have visited the village, and after seeing her memorial in the church are usually persuaded to boost the coffers with generous insertions in the wall Gift Box. Mrs John Rolfe, alias Princess Pocahontas, served Heacham well and her image is carved on the village sign. Centuries later generations of the Rolfes were to become inextricably entwined through marriage with the Black family when Frances, the sister of Charles Neville Rolfe, married the Reverend Robert Couper Black. Both of them were steeped in Evangelicalism and took religious observance to a level that was extreme even by Victorian standards.

All objects other than those with biblical connotations had to be put away in cupboards on Saturday evenings, so that the eyes of the family should not alight on anything impure on the Sabbath. After church each Sunday, the Black family would not engage in any of the usual social exchanges, and only the Bible could be read in the afternoon. Nonetheless, they were by no means reclusive and Church House was for sixty years the venue for Sunday tea parties, to which members of the Rolfe and Black families could come uninvited. The four Black children were brought up in strict observance of their parents' missionary zeal, and Church House was the family home from 1860. Bessie, the eldest, had been born disabled in 1855 and had a restricted childhood marked by ill health but from which she gradually recovered. Her sisters Helen and Roberta, born in 1857 and 1862, were strong and healthy. As children of an impoverished clergyman, they were encouraged to earn a living when they grew up and accordingly Helen, rather more broadminded than her siblings, trained as a nurse in London. Their brother Raymond Charles followed his father's calling and was ordained priest, serving in various parishes before relinquishing his living in London to become Rector of Stanhoe and Vicar of Barwick, the two neighbouring villages of Heacham from 1902-1932. As Rural Dean of Heacham from 1909-1924, he and his wife Grace lived in the village, and in 1939 celebrated his 60 years in the Ministry. His three sisters remained spinsters. After the death of their parents Church House became, and remained for half a century, the focal point for the Rolfe and Black families to meet for the customary Sunday tea parties when American visitors, researching their ancestry back to Princess Pocahontas, were also warmly welcomed.

Helen's nursing career, short lived though it was, was to change not just her life but also that of her sister Bessie as well as many of the poorer people of Heacham. Whilst working in the boroughs of Westminster and Paddington, she became aware of the impoverished lives of destitute children and orphans in state institutions, as well as in those of the Church of England Children's Society or Dr Barnado's homes.

The good Doctor, a pioneer in his field, had always believed that children were best cared for within a family environment rather than institutions. With that in mind he introduced the 'boarding out' system, an early form of fostering. In 1887 three hundred and thirty boys were sent to live with poor but respectable families who were obliged to treat them as they would their own family. Having established that they were devout Christians, clean living and kind, they would be inspected on a regular basis and would be paid five shillings a week for the keep of a child, provided that they were not in any way motivated by 'the greed of gain.' Dr Barnardo himself had originally been motivated by missionary zeal and had gone to London in order to qualify in medicine before going to China as an evangelical medical missionary. So affected was he by the destitute children that he encountered in the slums that he resolved to help them instead.

The population explosion in Victorian London following the Industrial Revolution, particularly in the East End, had resulted in overcrowded slums where extreme poverty, unemployment, and disease were rampant. One child in five died before its fifth birthday. Dr Barnado, the fourth of the six children of a Dublin couple, John and Abigail Barnado, was, by the time he was 25, the founder of a charity that was to transform the lives of thousands of children and to spawn other similar charities. His boarding-out policy became widespread, and children from London institutions were sent out to country families wherever possible. Helen soon became involved in this, and co-opted Bessie to help the cause in Norfolk, forming the Heacham Boarding Out Committee. From 1912-1921 Bessie was the Secretary, diligently performing her duties in arranging and supervising the placements of children. By the time she died in 1936 aged eighty-one, 200 children had passed through her hands. Few local people were aware of the extent of her good works, although the sisters were known to be devout ladies whose Christian faith was demonstrated in deeds as well church attendance.

Miss Black, as she was known in the village, was a familiar figure in Heacham. With no children of her own she was aware that there were families in her village who struggled to live in impoverished circumstances on very little money. If they were God-fearing church-goers or chapel goers perhaps they could be persuaded to foster needy children from homes in London. Those placed with Heacham families would be known as 'Miss Black's children'. That way they might be happily fostered, and the families with whom they were placed provided with extra income from funds raised either from charitable donors, or from the London County Council.

The children placed in Norfolk by the Blacks were amongst the lucky ones. Following legislation in 1850, local authorities were sanctioned to send children in large numbers to Canada, a scheme that Dr Barnado endorsed. In 1882 fifty one of his boys left Stepney, followed by another hundred boys and seventy-two girls the following year. By the turn of the century the charity was sending up to a thousand children a year under a mass migration scheme. As was the case at home, the rules were supposedly strict. Churchgoing and school were obligatory and children must be treated as family by their foster parents. But supervision was difficult considering the vast distances covered, and the harsh winters. Thus exploitation was inevitable. Boys over 13 were sent to farms where in many instances they were used as slave labour. The same fate awaited many of the girls that were put into Canadian domestic service, where they were ill used and overworked. With the limited media coverage at that time the scandal remained largely unheard of. Nonetheless child migration to Canada was suspended during the First World War, which was when the services of the Black sisters were greatly welcomed.

Bessie Black was diligent in what she came to regard as her most important work. As well as overseeing children that she had already boarded out, she was constantly on the lookout for prospective foster parents, particularly if they were impoverished.

One such family was the Gotsells. William, a retired gardener lived with his wife Sarah and daughter Ada in a small rented cottage in Pound Lane, Heacham. They had been pleased to foster a companion, Ethel, for their only child and would, now that she had left home to go into domestic service, probably consider welcoming another. Mrs Gotsell had herself been in domestic service and kept a tidy home. Being a practising Methodist she attended Chapel every Sunday, as well as Church, as was expected of her by her husband who was equally devout, albeit Church of England. They too were Victorians, instilled with the strict moral code of that era, and shocked at anything that might be considered wanton behaviour. Yes, Miss Black resolved to approach the Gotsells again and see if they would oblige her by providing a home for another of 'her children' when the time was ripe. They were elderly by this time but that should not be an impediment, and having a little extra money would surely ease their journey into old age.

Their front room was used only on Sundays or when visitors called. The back parlour with the black cooking range complete with flat irons, was where Mrs Gotsell worked and where the family ate at a table which was never without a clean cloth. There was no plumbing, electricity or water. Every drop had to be drawn from the outside pump, carried indoors, heated on the range, used, and carried from the house to be tipped out. Filling, heating and emptying the double-handled galvanised tub for the weekly bath which took place in the middle of the room was something of a ritual as well as an ordeal.

The large backyard housed a shed full of Mr Gotsell's gardening tools, all well worn after years of use growing flowers and vegetables, and at the end of the path was the privy. Long before the days of Bronco, let alone the loo rolls of today, torn papers hung from a string. Once a week the horse-drawn 'Honeycart' called under cover of darkness to empty all the cottage pails, and what might not be seen

Mrs Gotsell outside Bolivia Cottage,
Pound Lane, Heacham (1918)

Bolivia Cottage as it is today

was definitely smelt. Two men undertook the task, neither well paid nor enjoyable, but who were they to complain? They didn't have to toil in daylight hours.

Bolivia Cottages in Pound Lane, built of the local carrstone, were considered quite a modern terrace in 1914, being a mere 25 years old, and built in typical Victorian style. Today the houses have all been modernised, stripped of their name in favour of numbering, and dollied up with the addition of porches and bathrooms. But they remain easily recognisable and still have their large back gardens with their privies at the end, still intact but put to different uses.

Chapter 6

During the years of the Great War, Heacham was bereft of its men, and the women, like so many throughout the nation, toiled in their absence. Life became sombre with little variation in activities and much emphasis on 'the war effort.' So notice of an impending visit from Miss Bessie Black in 1917 prompted much speculation as well as preparation.

Sarah Gotsell opened up the front room, unwrapped the best china tea set and cleaned the cottage even more thoroughly than usual. Whatever could it be that prompted such an occasion? Surely she wouldn't suggest that they should foster another child now that they were getting on a bit and Ethel had left home? After somewhat stilted greetings all was revealed.

"I'm sure you know that there are still many destitute children being looked after in institutions in London", Miss Black began. "The scheme that Dr Barnado introduced for children to be boarded out in the country has proved to be very popular, but many more foster parents are still needed. I've helped to place many such children and as Ethel Townsend's placement with you was so successful I wonder if you'd consider having another child now that Ethel has left home?"

Predictably this proposal needed careful consideration, and when Miss Black left, Mrs Gotsell promised to discuss it with her husband. Together they would make a decision. Another meeting was arranged at which a certain misgiving was raised. Although the money would be a help, there was the question of clothes. Would there be extra funds as there had been for Ethel or would they be required to provide them from the five shillings a week fostering money? Miss Black reassured them.

"No, certainly not. If you decide to have a little girl, and I have one in mind called Mary Church who's three years old, all her clothes will be provided. I'll call once a month, and if you lay everything out on her bed we can discuss what's needed and I'll give you the money to replace things".

There was another problem. Age. When the Gotsells had agreed to foster Ethel they had been much younger. But at 61 Mr Gotsell was no longer a fit man, and his wife at 57 not altogether sure that she could manage so young a child. By the time she became a teenager, they would both be old. But of course it might be nice to have someone young who could help with household tasks, and even care for them in later years. But who was Mary Church and why was she in a children's home?

"Unfortunately I can tell you very little about her beyond the fact that she's a pretty child with fair hair and a lovely smile. According to those who look after her, she's

St Mary-le-Strand, London

no trouble. She's been at the home since she was about two months old, but no one knows who her parents are. She was found well wrapped up and in good health on December 13th 1914, abandoned on the steps of St Mary-le-Strand Church in the City of London. Nobody came to claim her, and nor did anyone see her being left there. All enquiries failed and so she was named after the church where she was found. There is a chance, of course, that she was illegitimate. But we mustn't dwell on that but think instead that perhaps

Mary aged 3 on arrival with foster parents Mr & Mrs Gotsell (1917)

extreme poverty forced her mother to make such a sacrifice in the hopes that her daughter might have a brighter future. And of course, being war time, her father might even have been killed in France and perhaps with other children to fend for, a baby was more than his widow could cope with".

It was tempting. Ethel, the first child that they had fostered as a companion for their only daughter had indeed left home. Ada was also out to work now in Lamberts the grocers in Snettisham, the next-door village, leaving home early each day to bicycle to work. On Saturdays she would seldom get home before seven, and in winter that meant a cold ride in the dark. The house did seem a bit empty now.

Yes: the Gotsells told Miss Black that they would welcome an addition to their family. It would be quite possible to put another bed in Ada's room and preparations were made. When Miss Black next went to London it was to fetch the little girl whose life was to change so radically. It must have been something of a trauma for a three year old to leave the security of the only home she had ever known, albeit an institution, to travel on a train, the likes of which she had never seen, and to do so with an elderly lady whom she did not know.

According to Ada's children, their mother knew little about the plan until on her return from work one day she found a small girl sitting by the kitchen range eating bread and jam.

"This is Mary, your new sister" she was told. Despite questioning her parents about the origins of this new sister, she gleaned no information. What Miss Black knew she never divulged, and the Gotsells, being somewhat subservient, never asked any of the questions that might have enlightened them all. It was the age when humble people did not question 'their betters.'

In Bessie Black's journal, meticulously kept during her tenure of duty, the accounts make interesting reading. 'Mary Church, foundling, arrived by train on 30th January 1918 aged 3 years.' There is no mention of where she came from, other than that it was London. She was always led to believe that it was from a Dr Barnado's home, but it may have been that the Gotsells had never heard of any other children's charity, and they would certainly not have been aware that there were council institutions. And so it was that Mary Church grew up, and indeed died, believing that she was a Barnado's child. Her keep for the year cost £33.8.2d which was drawn from the Guardians Savings Account. Her board at 5/- per week amounted to £26.9s.2d. Clothing £3, her Sunday best outfit £2.10s, the Doctor £1, reports and incidentals 8s. and her Christmas gift (presumably the book) 1s. Hardly luxury living. But there were no adverse reports registered against her name, as was the case with a poor little boy called Richard, whose 'habits rendered it impossible to keep him.' There were three

Mary Church's foster parents William and Sarah Gotsell (1920)

other Heacham children who were contemporaries of Mary Church, all of them in children's homes since babyhood. Charles Spencer was found abandoned in Wardour Street, Soho; Enid Stone was born in Wallis Yard Workhouse, and Edward Cross was left at Charing Cross Station. Mary Church was the only one of them whose origins were not known and who never knew her proper name. Despite her exhaustive enquiries in later years she drew a blank and was not even able to find out any details of where she had spent the first three years of her life. So why did she not ask Miss Black?

"Oh, I couldn't have done that. She would have told me if she had thought I should know". The subservience which had been so instilled in her by the Gotsells was hard to overcome. Miss Black, kind and charitable as she was, would have seemed a formidable figure to a young girl. Or maybe there was a reluctance to delve if there was any likelihood that by doing so she might be opening Pandora's box.

Happily the newly introduced sisters seemed to settle down to their shared existence, not that they saw a great deal of each other. Ada was just another grown-up rather than a playmate for Mary. She was an old lady when I knew her on the annual visit that she paid to stay with her sister at School Lane, Rockland St Mary. Nanny had always spoken of her as Mrs Flint and I did likewise. Had I known what a wealth of information she could have given me about the young Mary Church, I would have tapped her memory. But she died before anything had been divulged Only her children, Tony and Joan, have been able to recount tales that she told them about the Gotsells' family life at Bolivia Cottage.

They knew that their aunt Mary was fun to have around when they were children, and that it was she who bought Joan her first bicycle. Joan also remembers a treasured pale blue skirt, jersey and matching beret that she had knitted for her. To her horror she fell over when wearing it and was far more concerned about the state of the outfit than her bleeding knees. Tony and Joan also remember her taking them to the cinema after much discussion as to its suitability for children. Even more enlightening was that their aunt Mary's boyfriend used to come and stay. We had never heard tell of romance beyond the fact that a cowman had once made unwelcome advances at Stibbard, but we felt sure there must have been others. Evidently the boyfriend referred to was around for some time before fading from the scene. The reserve that was to be Mary's lifelong armour was probably already in evidence. It's been my good fortune that Nanny's family, and in particular Joan, has been able to fill in many of the gaps in the

Heacham School 1921 (Mary - Middle Row, 5th from right)

story as well as providing photographs. And it's been an added bonus that all of them have encouraged me to write this. They too appreciate that the story of Mary Church is one that should be told. But romance? No, even in her youth she 'kept herself to herself'.

Years later our postman, Mr Morley, used to linger over cups of coffee with her, resulting in much teasing. It didn't go unnoticed that he brought our post earlier and earlier, and stayed longer and longer. Nanny would always good naturedly retort 'get away with you' when the children asked her if she'd be meeting Mr Morley in Norwich on her day off. With a giggle she would grudgingly admit that "Well, mmmm... he's quite nice, but I'm not interested". In fact her 'quite nice' was the nearest she ever got to a superlative.

Only since she died have I been able to pursue her life story, and

Mary Church aged 5

Heacham seemed the obvious place to start. There are still people in the village, albeit old, whose memories remain sharp which has been my good fortune. One such person, Mrs Margaret Skoyles, a diminutive and chatty octogenarian, was as welcoming as she was delighted to talk about old times.

"Oh yes, I knew Mary Church. We used to play together, all of us children did because we all lived near each other. It was hopscotch or skipping ropes and if a horse and cart came along the road outside where we always played, we just lay the rope on the ground until it had driven past". Today her house in Meadow Lane, just round the corner from Pound Lane, is surrounded by new development, and it's more than the odd horse and cart that speeds past her door.

"We all went to the village school until we were 14, except for the few that got scholarships and went to King Edward's at King's Lynn. We had wonderful teachers but oh my word they were strict. There was Mr Suter and then Mr Quayle who lived in the School House. Then there was Miss Hulme. She was single you know, because in those days teachers had to be really dedicated. If they got married they had to give up. Yes, that was the rule then".

I wondered what discipline was like, and what punishments were meted out?

"Oh, the cane of course" she said with a giggle. "We had to hold our hands out and it used to sting. But I don't think it did anyone any harm and it certainly made us pay attention and behave. Nothing like all that rudeness and bad behaviour that you hear about today. I don't reckon children nowadays know the meaning of discipline, and a great pity too. But what can you expect with all their mothers out to work and teachers not allowed to punish? They tell me that they're not allowed to touch children, even when they fall over and hurt themselves. Something to do with being sued. Whatever next?"

Margaret Skoyles proceeded to drive a coach and horses through 'all this nonsense about what you call it – political correctness, whatever that is". She was particularly eloquent about "all them interfering busybodies from the Council and that'.

Was there a school uniform of any sort, I wondered, as I attempted to steer her away from what was clearly her current hobby horse.

'The boys all wore short trousers, whatever the weather, until they left school, and we girls used to wear pinafores over our dresses to keep them clean. Most of us wore lace-up boots if our parents could afford them – they were expensive, mind, but they lasted a good long time, and when they got holes in them the village cobbler used to mend them. There weren't any washing machines and our mothers had to wash everything by hand with carbolic soap, and beat the really dirty things on the washboard in the outside shed. Some people had a mangle, but if not you just wrung everything out and hung it on the line. We used to heat up water in a copper on the range. There was no electricity until the mid 30's, so school used to finish in daylight and then at home we had paraffin lamps or candles'.

"Did children ever go out from the village?" I asked.

"No, not really; there was no transport except trains. It wasn't like it is now with everyone having cars. We all had second hand bicycles which were handed down, and we used to ride down to the river or to the beach. Of course there wasn't crime like there is today, and there was certainly no need for all these social workers and counsellors and what have you. We all had neighbours and we all looked after each other. It was a much better life then, even if we were much poorer. We didn't ever need to lock our doors. Good gracious no. People were honest in those days and anyway what would there have been worth stealing? We left school at 14 and not just at the end of the term either. We left on the day of our 14th birthday. We weren't sophisticated like the teenagers of today, but we knew how to behave all right and we all knew how to read and write properly. Schoolchildren used to be very well taught".

I told her that Mary Church had always said that Sundays were the highlight of the week.

"Oh yes, they were wonderful. We all put on our Sunday best - everyone, no matter how poor they were had their Sunday best, and first of all the children went to Sunday School with Miss Helen Black. Then it was church, or chapel for the Methodists. Then in the afternoon we went to Bible class with Mrs Black, the wife of the Reverend; and then it was choir practice and after that church again for Evensong. Mary couldn't sing very well so she wasn't in the choir".

Correct, but she could belt out a recognisable nursery rhyme without any trouble.

"Mary was my patrol leader in White Heather".

"In what?"

"The Guides. She was older than me and very good at sewing, and she got all her badges. Miss Brown who took Guides each Friday made her leader so that she could teach all of us in her patrol".

I told Mrs Skoyles that although her friend Mary had been with my family for 43 years, she had never told me much about her childhood in Heacham, even though I had tried to get her to talk about it.

"Well Mary was always a bit reserved. I think it was because she was one of Miss Black's girls and had been in Barnado's or some such place before she

Sunday best, aged 6 (1920)

came to Heacham. But there were quite a lot of them and they were all very popular. But they definitely felt different somehow, not having their own parents. Then of course Mary's were quite old and rather severe. She was a wonderful daughter to them later on". A choice of career for the children of Heacham Village School was unheard of in the 20's and 30's. Poor wages and the recession did nothing for improving prosperity. For girls it was domestic service or shop assistant if they were lucky, and for the boys, farm work. Surprisingly then, the village was home to several eminent people, with Patrick Hadleigh, composer and Professor of Music at Cambridge University even deemed worthy of a plaque on the wall surrounding his house. Cambridge University, and in particular Gonville and Caius College were pivotal to Heacham, as they were on a much humbler scale to Mary Church who was to spend ten years there, first as under housemaid and then as parlour-maid.

Chapter 7

It was in 1869 that Martin Davy, Master of Caius College, who lived with his family in the Master's Lodge, decided to buy 200 acres of land in Heacham, together with a splendid Queen Anne house. This was to be used as a country retreat. A Trust was set up which stipulated that for the privilege of having such a house, he and future Masters would be required to finance its upkeep with income from the farm and to spend at least 60 days a year there. It may be assumed that academics then as now are not usually well versed in the vagaries of country living let alone farming, so it is hardly surprising to learn that successive Masters of Caius struggled to fulfil their obligations to what became known as Heacham Lodge. From 1869 until 1933 it did function as had been intended.

In 1928 James Cameron became Master. Married to an extremely hospitable Quaker wife who delighted in entertaining all comers, both the Lodge in Cambridge and the one in Heacham soon resembled Friends Meeting Houses. With a growing family as well as constant guests, Mrs Cameron needed a large domestic staff, which included seven maids, as well as a cook and housekeeper in The Master's Lodge in Cambridge, a rabbit warren of a house. College functions, which took place in the Dining Hall, required extra staff, including a butler who was also responsible for teaching novice maids such tasks as buffing up the huge array of college silver which would adorn the high table. The domestic staff, being predominantly female, had for years been known as 'the bed makers' and at Christmas time the annual staff treat was known as The Bed Makers' Party. The Master and his family were expected to perform some sort of play following which everyone joined in the dancing. It lasted from 8 o'clock until midnight and if it was hardly an alcoholic binge, it was a very jolly affair with the house being the perfect setting for games of sardines.

As Mary's 14th birthday approached, the Gotsells were paid a special visit by Miss Black to plan her future employment. I don't think there can have been much discussion as I remembered Nanny telling me "Miss Black put me into service in Cambridge. She didn't ask me if I'd like to go or such like, but because I was one of her girls I knew that I had to go where she told me". Did she ask any questions about payment, or what she would have to do? "Oh dear me, no. I was just very grateful to have a job at all. I always knew that what Miss Black arranged, happened".

Mr and Mrs Cameron were good friends of Miss Black's due to the fact that they spent much time at their house in Heacham. Mary would go to work for them as an under housemaid and would live in with the rest of the staff. She would be provided with two sets of uniform, one of which would be for mornings when she would be cleaning and polishing, and the other would be a black dress with white apron and cap into which she would change for the afternoons when she would be available for any tasks which Mrs Cameron might need to be done. She would be paid £15 a year and would, of course, have all her keep. She would have one half day off each week. Because the household came to stay in The Lodge at Heacham during the holidays, she would be able to see her family and friends then.

It was with foreboding that the rather shy and sheltered 14 year-old set off by train to Cambridge with Miss Black, her meagre possessions packed into a cheap cardboard case. She, who had never left home and had dreaded doing so, was now confronted with painful farewells. But even then, Mary Church's upbringing had ensured that there would be no hysterics or even resentment. It was just one of those things. It was time for her to leave home and go into service and perhaps she was one of the lucky ones. Not all of Miss Black's girls were able to return to Heacham during the holidays. Mary's first resolve was to see if she could send some of the money that she would be earning to her parents, both of whom were now frail and old. It was 1928.

Initially, overwhelmed by the sheer size of the city and of the College, the new maid did not venture out at all for several weeks. Her room which she shared with three others was spartan and cold and situated in the attics where all the household staff were housed. The house was so much larger than anything that she had been used to. Instead of drawing water from the Pound Lane pump and carrying it into the house, she was carting huge jugs up to the washstands in all the bedrooms each morning so that the Cameron family and their guests could wash. The maids had to be up by 6.30, dressed in their working dress with aprons and caps. The fireplaces had to be cleaned and re-laid and the grates black-leaded and polished. Logs and coal needed replenishing, and, if the fire did not instantly light when struck with a match, whoever had laid it would be reprimanded. Firelighters and central heating were not yet part of College life. Next, the stairs had to be swept before the Master, his family or houseguests used them. Should a servant find herself on the stairs when one of them appeared, she must quickly vanish.

It was important to observe the pecking order of servants 'below stairs' and Mary was the lowliest, on a par with the kitchen maids. Parlour-maids were next in seniority. They had got their promotion through dint of hard work and a kindly housekeeper who, if she did not like you, could make life extremely difficult. So how did Mary endear herself? Talking about her days at Cambridge was never a problem.

"I got on alright. I think she quite liked me because I used to help her with the linen cupboard, even though that was really the sewing maid's job. But she knew I was good at sewing. We all had a good time even though we had to work hard".

The Camerons, by the sound of it, ran a happy household and the staff had little to complain of. They all ate in the servants' hall and soon got to know the sound of whichever bell rang to summon them. If it was during a mealtime then it meant leaving the table at once and probably returning when the food was cold. After lunch when the tables had been cleared and the washing up done by the kitchen maids, the staff were free for a couple of hours which Mary evidently spent in her room. As she grew in confidence, so she started to enjoy all that was around her. When the Master was dining in Hall the maids used to snoop from the gallery above and eavesdrop on the conversation. She was honest enough to admit, and indeed told me, "Of course it was all way above our heads. There was always grace to start off with before anyone sat down, and it was all in Latin. We had to be careful not to get the giggles. It was lovely seeing the Master and all the Fellows dressed up in their white tie and tails and the waiters who came in for the evening all wore white gloves and stood against the wall. And the silver was really sparkling in the candlelight".

So what about the churchgoing that Miss Black and the Gotsells had always insisted on?

"Oh we all went to college chapel every Sunday. We usually had to listen to some quite long sermons. Learned people used to come to preach and they were always very long-winded".

When the holidays arrived and it was time to set off for Norfolk, a

Freda England, Mary Church (2002)

crocodile of staff headed for the station loaded with luggage to board the train for King's Lynn, followed by another to Heacham. The Lodge there became home for several weeks at a time, and an altogether more relaxed atmosphere prevailed. The Black sisters always called, and during her time off in the afternoons Mary was able to visit her old home to see her foster parents. To her delight, Freda Alcock, another Heacham girl who had been fostered and then adopted, joined the Lodge staff. They had been at school together as well as in the Guides. 70 years later when I took Nanny back to Heacham for one of her annual birthday treats, while we were wandering in the churchyard looking for the Gotsells graves there was suddenly a shriek. "Mary!" We looked round to see a small grey haired old lady coming towards us.

"Mary. You remember me?"

"No" replied Nanny.

"It's Freda. Surely you remember? We were at school together and in the Guides and then we both worked at the Lodge. I was Freda Alcock and now I'm Freda England. I'm a churchwarden now so I'm just here to sort out some newsletters. Fancy seeing you here".

Mercifully Nanny's memory came sluggishly to life, shamelessly aided by me, and she did remember and was even quite forthcoming as the two of them exchanged reminiscences.

Freda had also been one of Miss Black's girls but Nanny explained to me that

The Lodge, Heacham

she was one of the lucky ones who knew who she was and where she had come from. She was also later adopted rather than fostered. Both of them had been in domestic service and both of them had worked together for the Camerons at Caius College, and at the Lodge. This seemed to me to be a good opportunity to talk about those early days in Heacham. But Nanny would have none of it. Her face puckered and her eyes filled with tears as she said, "It's no good. I just get upset when I think about it all".

We had just come from a visit to the Lodge where, despite her remonstrances not to do so, I had rung the doorbell and found myself confronting an extremely friendly and welcoming Austrian owner. Explaining that I had with me a former housemaid who had worked in his house seventy odd years ago, I was immediately bidden to bring her in. Her reaction was so typical – over anxious that our visit might be inconvenient, she didn't want to be a nuisance, and all but apologising for my appalling cheek in orchestrating such an intrusion. Nevertheless, she was interested to hear that the house had changed hands and was no longer anything to do with the College, although some of the land still belonged to Caius. The present Master no longer came to stay in Heacham but he was still the trustee of the Village Charity, which is responsible for the playing fields, tennis courts, and many other village amenities. As we walked round downstairs her comments coloured our tour, and her presence must have astonished our host.

"There's still the same fireplace. I used to blacklead that. Mrs Cameron didn't have any of that fancy wallpaper. The kitchen is quite different. The range used to be there. I wonder where that's gone. And the scullery isn't there any more, or the butler's pantry. We didn't use the front stairs of course, only the back stairs, sort of thing. That was the Master's Study". Her particular horror was the fact that all the surrounding fields seemed to have been built over.

After visiting the church, our final visit was to Bolivia Cottages, Pound Lane, where I took a photograph of the old lady standing outside the front of her childhood home. It was a nostalgic day and the one time that Nanny and I were able to talk about her past, as long as we kept to generalities. It was then that she said, "When anything happens to me" (wonderful avoidance of 'when I die') I'd like to have my funeral in Heacham Church. And I think there'll be plenty of money and such like because I've saved up to pay for it".

I assured her that she'd have the send-off she deserved.

Chapter 8

When she was 18, Mary was made a parlour-maid. Her pay was increased by £5 a year, much of which she was able to save and give to her foster parents. She had by her own admission blossomed in the service of the Camerons. Her new duties meant that she was rather less 'below stairs' and more in evidence 'above stairs.' She was now responsible for such things as serving tea in the drawing room where Mrs Cameron entertained her many friends. The Master's Study similarly became her responsibility, not that she was ever allowed to touch or move anything. There were constant comings and goings of Fellows, Dons, and undergraduates during term time, as well as visitors from other colleges. Instead of her formerly reclusive life,

Aged 18, Caius College parlour-maid

Caius College Cambridge, Staff Outing, 1938
Mary Church (head & shoulders) seated on ground right of centre, her feet showing in front.

Mary ventured out during her free time, either walking or bicycling all over the town. She got on well with all the household staff bar one whom she described as "a real menace. I think she was jealous that I was a parlour-maid and she seemed set on getting me into trouble. But she had to leave because she got herself in the family way".

That sounded as if life in the College had its moments. Were there some troublesome men there I had enquired, wondering if there was a revelation forthcoming.

"Yes, some of the young men who were supposed to be studying got quite fresh, but they didn't get anywhere with me. Of course there weren't any girl students in those days".

What today might sound like sheer domestic drudgery seemed to have no such connotations in the twenties and thirties. Try as I might, I never got the reaction that I expected, and had to conclude that if there were armies of militant domestic servants waiting for the day when a trade union would free them from serfdom and exploitation, they were not to be found at Gonville and Caius College. On the contrary. The staff there, and presumably in many other households, considered themselves fortunate to have secure jobs where their keep was provided and life was good. But what of the old servants who would have no pensions when they retired, let alone any social services to apply to for benefits.

"Well, it all depended on your employer. Good ones used to look after their staff, sometimes for the rest of their lives, and give them cottages to live in rent-free. But of course there were stories of hardship, especially when an employer died, leaving servants with nowhere to go".

It sounded to me as if life was all work and very little leisure.

"I suppose you could say that we all had a different attitude to the youngsters of today. Television didn't exist so we never saw advertisements for things that we couldn't afford, and although the pay by modern standards was very low, we all thought we were lucky to have jobs that we enjoyed. And we definitely took great pride in our work. Elbow grease was what we most needed and nowadays you won't find many young girls who know what that means. And the other thing that was different was that we didn't go shopping unless we really needed something that was worn out, and which we would have saved up for. When I went home my mother used to get me to unpick my father's trousers and jacket when they were getting a bit worn, and turn them and sew them together the other way round. And I used to turn his collars and cuffs too on his shirts. That wasn't at all unusual and then they would last a whole lot longer".

William Gotsell died in 1936, leaving his wife Sarah in failing health. Dutifully their foster daughter Mary took leave from her job in Cambridge to return to Heacham to look after her until she too died in 1938. Miss Bessie Black had died in 1936, so her sister, Miss Helen Black, with no doubt the kindest of intentions, wrote as follows:

> *Dear Mary,*
>
> *I write to you on the death of your mother to express my sympathy. Of course it means that now you will be without a home. I hope it will give you comfort to remember that Our Lord always looks kindly on the poor and lonely. You will always remember what a good and dutiful daughter you were.*
>
> *Yours sincerely,*
>
> *Helen Black*

Although she was something of a squirrel, keeping obsolete knitting or sewing patterns and piles of postcards sent to her by her children, this was among the very few letters that she kept all her life, safely stored in an aged envelope. There were two others. One was from the London County Council Public Assistance Department written to Miss Black when Mary was sixteen years old. Under the title Adoption, it informed her that *'on the 21st instant it was decided that the Education Department shall exercise the rights and powers of parents in respect of Mary Church 5W 22108 pursuant to the provisions of Section 52(i) of the Poor Law Act 1930.'*

Mary had been adopted, not by the Gotsells, but by a department in far off Buckingham Palace Road.

In fact she was not entirely homeless. Her sister Ada, with her husband Cecil and their two children told her she would always be welcome in their home should she ever need it.

It may not have been the most extensive or even systematic research, but Mary did make a concerted effort to trace her origins. She visited St Mary le Strand Church but found the experience too traumatic to linger, and did not instigate any enquiries there. When I visited it I could quite understand why a mother would choose such a place to leave her baby. The stone steps leading up to the doors are wide and in full view of the busy Strand which divides into two lanes to pass the island in the middle of which stands the church. Mary's mother would have been in no doubt that the small bundle would be spotted, hopefully by a kind churchgoer who would see that she was put into good hands.

I probed further, asking the attendant lady for the name and telephone number of someone who would be able to help me with the history and records of the church. One of the churchwardens, a historian currently writing a book on the subject, was just the person. He had a fund of information about London in general, and St Mary's and the Strand in particular, but regrettably could uncover no details about the baby girl that was found on the church steps in 1914. He told me that records of the early 20th century were lamentably scarce, it being an era when at the end of an incumbency the outgoing Vicar tended to clear away all but parish registers and important diocesan papers. He could find no mention of the church's namesake. But there was ample evidence of such practices in earlier centuries and in the 17th century when Pepys was chronicling life in London. Babies were frequently abandoned, particularly if they were illegitimate or born into a pauper's family. It was the custom then, and remained so into the eighteenth and nineteenth centuries, to name babies according to the place where they were found, so evidently the custom had continued into the twentieth century. The most unusual name that he had come across was that of a boy called Oilbut who had presumably been found either in or on one. St Mary-le-Strand still administers a charity set up with the proceeds of the sale of seven acres of land alongside the Kent Road in the seventeenth century. Its purpose then remains the same today – to ease the plight of the poor who live or did live in the area. Ironically, many of the recipients of money from the fund have been retired domestic servants whose employers made no provision for them once their working lives were over.

Had Mary felt able to identify herself to the Vicar or church-wardens of the day, instead of being somewhat overcome with the emotion of it all, she would undoubtedly have been greatly welcomed. They would have been as interested to hear her story, as was the churchwarden of today. Furthermore, nearly 70 years ago as it was, there just might have been a reference to her which had survived the clearing of desks.

Mary's next attempt to unearth her past was to write to the London County Council whom she knew had adopted her, asking them if they had any details of her early life. And that was the end of her attempts to identify herself. The reply which came back was stark and probably as typical a letter from a civil servant as might be written today.

> *Dear Madam,*
>
> *Referring to your letter of the 28th instant I have to inform you that the only information I can find on the records is that you were found at St Mary-le-Strand Church on 13th December 1914. At that time you were judged to be about 2 months old.*
>
> *I regret that I am unable to give you any information about your parents.*
>
> *I hope you are comfortable and happy in your present position and will continue so during the useful career which you have in front of you.*

Her useful career was that of a domestic servant at Gonville and Caius College.

And so the first three years of her life remained a mystery, never to be unfolded during her lifetime. She never knew which home she had been taken to, or even where in London it was. Her quest for an identity came to an abrupt end and she simply assumed that she had been 'A Barnado's child.'

Today it is far easier to unravel the past and with the freedom of information afforded to us we should have little difficulty finding, in the case of adopted children, real parents, and in instances of institutional life the actual establishment where years were spent.

I knew that in her will Mary had left £1000 to both The Children's Society and Barnado's, so as executor of her will it was always my intention when sending them their cheques to ask them to trace Mary Church and to tell me where in London she had spent the first three years of her life. Back came two disappointing replies. Both charities were very grateful for their legacies, but neither of them could find any trace of her. Strange indeed. Equally strange was the fact that her nephew Tony and his wife, believing that their aunt was a Barnado's child, adopted two coloured boys from one of their London homes. Mary always told them that, like her, they were lucky to have been Barnado's children and equally lucky to have been taken on by loving families. Either the charity records were incomplete, or Mary had been fed false information. She clearly believed what she had been told and when her quest for further information hit the buffers, she simply got on with her life. It was just one of those things. But it hurt.

Always the bridesmaid, never the bride.

Sister Ada's wedding

Ethel & Jock's wedding (1934)
Ethel was the first child to be fostered by the Gotsells.

Extensive research has failed to reveal the identity of the bridal couple.
(Mary Church on the right)

Chapter 9

I've often heard how for some people war was a great opportunity to escape the boredom of a dreary lifestyle and head for adventure. So it was for Mary. Not for her the life of a land girl or a munitions worker. She set her sights on joining the WAAF, and as East Anglia was peppered with RAF stations she thought she'd be in with a chance. She was 27 years old when on November 5th 1941 she headed for the recruiting office in Norwich to sign on. Weeks later she became No. 2013243 WAAF Mary Church, Aircrafthand/Balloon Operator.

"I had a bit of trouble choosing which trade I wanted to join because the officer who interviewed me seemed to think that because I had been in domestic service I'd work in the cookhouse. I told him I was definitely not prepared to do that, and I wanted to learn something new. So they signed me up to train first of all as a balloon operator and then after I'd done that for two years, as a Mechanical Transport Mechanic. As I couldn't even drive and had only ever done a few puncture repairs on my bike, it was quite a challenge".

Spanners replaced the silver spoons of Caius College, and overalls the apron and cap. As for thinking that she would be spending all her time in Norfolk, it was not to be. During her five years service she had postings to Morecambe, Gloucester, Portreath and Buchan, serving with three different squadrons – No's 925, 927 and 945.

2013243 WAAF Mary Church

"It was amazing really because I'd had such a sheltered life and suddenly there I was travelling all over the country and seeing places that I'd only ever read about. Mind you, one RAF station in wartime was much the same as any other. Everything was in camouflage and the discipline was very strict".

Was she a good mechanic? I found it difficult to visualise her very small hands blackened by oil, brandishing spanners.

"Well I got by. I learnt how to strip down a diesel engine and when I put it together the wrong way the Flight Sergeant made me do it over and over again until I got so that I could even do it in the dark by torchlight. We always had to be able to do that because of the blackout. But I never did anything to an aeroplane. I got demoted once and lost a stripe but I soon got it back and by the time I was demobbed I was Leading Aircraftwoman with two stripes".

So what had operating a balloon to do with stripping down diesel engines?

"Nothing at all. In fact I had two trades. To start with I was on a station where the barrage balloons had to be winched up whenever the siren went to tell us that there was an air raid coming, and winched down again after the all clear. They didn't come right down of course because they were fixed in position, and the ones I worked on were on top of a hill. They were supposed to make it difficult for the German bombers to come low enough to be accurate at hitting their targets because if they did, they might get ensnared in the wire hawsers and the balloons. The trouble was that it was nearly always night work. We worked in teams so that when we had to scramble, we all knew exactly where to go to our positions. Actually, although it was hard work we had a lot of fun. But I was quite glad when I got posted and changed to being a mechanic".

Four years and two months after she enlisted, Leading Aircraftwoman Mary Church was discharged from the RAF on January 10th 1946, the possessor of two medals and listed as Class A Reserve. Fifty years later that was to have very significant and extremely funny repercussions.

It was because of the Lapsleys that WAAF Mary Church became a nanny. The Squadron Leader was a Battle of Britain pilot and his wife was a WAAF officer. They knew that Mary had been in domestic service, so they asked her if she would like to look after their two children after the war.

"It was a very good offer because otherwise I had no idea what I would be going back to. They had two small children Peter and Penny and I went to work for them at Horsham St Faith RAF Station near Norwich and had some very happy years with them. I stayed until Peter went away to boarding school and leaving them was really dreadful. I made a bad mistake then and went to work for a family where the mother didn't seem to trust me with the children and used to spy on me. I was so unhappy there that after about a year Mrs Lapsley rescued me and I went back to them until I got another job. That was at Oundle School working for one of the housemasters. I was happy there. The Beresfords were a nice family and I stayed with them until I went back to Norfolk to the Ashworths when James was born. I could have stayed there even after James had gone away to school, but it would have been to look after Mr Ashworth's elderly mother, and I really wanted to get back to looking after a baby again".

The parting must have been awful after having looked after James for so long.

"It was. I really dreaded leaving him but he was the last of the family. His elder brother and sister were already away at boarding school so when James went, I knew that I must go. That's how it is with nannies though. The time always comes to part with children that you've grown so fond of. You get over it, but it's hard, really hard. You see, the children I've looked after have seemed like my children, so leaving them really hurt. But as I always say, it's just one of those things, like that song about nannies. I can't remember the words except the line 'mother to dozens but nobody's wife'".

Well, maybe. But as Nanny was at the end rather than the beginning of her career, hopefully she'd stay with us.

Chapter 10

1989

Happy in the knowledge that I would not be leaving Nanny permanently behind in Rockland St Mary, and having completed the purchase of my new house, things seemed to be looking up. I had overcome the uncontrollable urge to cry every time anyone mentioned my imminent move, so that far from it being the daunting and deeply depressing event that I had envisaged it became something of an adventure. Builders were soon virtually gutting the place and I, having decided not to employ an architect, was engrossed in the daily dismemberment that was taking place before the refurbishment could begin. A thick black marker pen became my trade tool as I wrote instructions on walls, doors, and windows. 'Demolish' featured prominently, easily interpreted by my eclectic collection of freelance tradesmen. Down came the wall in the hall, down came the partition dividing the drawing room into two mean rooms, out came four badly warped sash windows, and away went two bedrooms, transformed into bathrooms. Up went Georgian cornicing, in went period fireplaces, and up went a conservatory. Demolition yards became my shopping venues and House and Garden magazine my chosen reading. When not actually overseeing the work in progress, I was driving back home to the sewing machine, making curtains and furnishings in abundance.

My sons' friends, promising to help, and suggesting themselves as weekend guests, were splendid company but useless workmen. One, of whom I was and remain very fond, abandoned his task of drilling a wall in order to fit a shelf, in favour of a quick kip in the bath where I found him fast asleep. Another, volunteering to shift hardcore from outside the front door, appeared after a mere ten minutes at his task asking for plasters for his blisters. Plasters were not something easily found on a building site, and so necessitated a walk to the shops.

Jeremy soon developed a latent talent for fixing curtain rails and pelmet boards, a skill that I'm sure will have subsequently stood him in good stead.

The actual move was something of a nightmare, which I had underestimated. What to do with thirty years of clobber and old toys, with canoes, bicycles, prams, saddlery, show jumps? I would tackle the barns and outbuildings; the boys could sort things out in the attics. Splendid idea, until I realised that they had been so delighted to be surrounded by boxes of discarded Lego that they had spent most of a precious weekend playing with it. The largest available skip was decided on and duly delivered to a strategic position outside the back door in the stable yard. Into it went every bit of flingable detritus, as well as a lot of outworn, outgrown, or outmoded garden tools, toys, kitchen utensils and general junk. Even two canoes. The removal men took the pain out of all the necessary packing of our precious possessions and finally, a year after buying the house in Swaffham, I moved into it.

One house at a time I had told myself and Nanny would have to wait a few months before I could get my head round to selling her house in Rockland and buying another one for her. When the moment did finally come, we all but came to blows. She came to stay so that she could view the shortlist, the particulars of which I had carefully sifted. Requirements? Proximity, a garden, scope for improvement and modernisation. The preference for something old meant that it was likely to be cold, damp and awkward, but the builders were set to start on renovations for her as soon as they had finished mine. But every single place that we visited seemed to fall short of the ideal, resulting in a dismissive sniff and "I don't think my sister would like it". Exasperated, I retorted, "Nanny, this house is for you, not your sister and she only comes to stay once a year, if that". Finally, furious, I said, "I'm not going to show you any more places. I'm going to buy one of them, do it all up for you and then show it to you".

And that was how 29 Cley Road, Swaffham, became the replacement for 5, School Lane, Rockland St Mary. It had a new kitchen, central heating, a big living room, a bedroom with adjoining bathroom, two little attic bedrooms and a garden. Nanny was totally charmed by it. She described it in her most expansive way as "Yes, quite nice". But there was what turned out to be something of a major problem. The wardrobe. She had a particularly unlovable cupboard in her bedroom at School Lane, and without it she could not and would not move. It had been there when she had first moved in, and part with it she would not. At first glance it seemed as if it would be a simple task. It could be taken to pieces, and lifted down the extremely narrow twisting stairs. Fine in theory, except that it didn't work. With

Mary with Kitty and Dominic, Jeremy and Georgie's children in the garden of her cottage, 29 Cley Road, Swaffham (1998)

Mary with Sister Ada (1990)

all concerned trying to get the various pieces downstairs, with verbal instructions increasing in volume, it was obvious that we had a major hitch. The wardrobe was in pieces; none of them would go through the window or down the stairs. Christopher, my son-in-law, had the answer. "We'll just have to take the stairs out". By the time he'd dismantled them slowly, tread by tread, he was less convinced of the brilliance of his suggestion, nor did his sense of humour prevail. It took a day to accomplish the removal of one thoroughly awkward wardrobe, and Christopher had yet to reassemble the stairs for the

incoming owners. What we had underestimated was the width of the staircase in Swaffham. It was even narrower and more twisting, there was no question of getting the cupboard up it and Christopher, despite his good nature, was in no mood to dismantle another set of stairs. Nanny merely remarked, "Oh well, it's just one of those things. I shall have to get a smaller wardrobe". She moved in happily. It took her five minutes to walk to my house, and almost as if there had been a mere blip instead of a major

80th Birthday

63

hiccup, life resumed its former pattern. She soon had the measure of sparkling up the brass and silver, but she couldn't 'find anything.' Where were the familiar coal tongs, the butter dish, and the woodchopper? I didn't care. Permanently up-ended in the garden, as long as I had the secateurs in my pocket and the wheelbarrow to hand I was happy.

But there were more cooking cremations than ever before. Now the possessor of an Aga, which never revealed tell tale smoke or smell, I had countless disasters. Strange really considering I had grown up with one, but thirty years of electricity had blunted my memory. Luckily, as the builders still dallied with the decorating, the smell of paint seemed to be more pervasive than that of burnt food. Bread was the worst and even now there are times when four loaves are transformed into rock solid black bricks.

The garden became my obsession and the Saturday market my new source of everything, plants, bulbs and shrubs in particular. Tyrone (named after the film star, of course) Roberts is a local celebrity with patter that's worth hearing even if you don't fancy buying anything. He had and still has me hooked. As the grandchildren have arrived, so I have bought superb old-fashioned large wheeled prams for £12, a sofa and chairs for a fiver and countless other things, many of which have been mistakes which have found their way straight back the following Saturday to the market from whence they came.

By the time Nanny's 80th birthday approached, and yes, this time I made sure that I had got the date right, both our houses were habitable. As well as having a housewarming party, the Hall family decided that we'd have a tea party for her and we'd start by inviting all her former charges. We soon overcame her initial protestations that she didn't want a party. Instead she was talking about buying a new dress and making an appointment for a perm, "So that I'll look alright for the party".

James Ashworth, who brought his wife, his parents and his sister, Karina, had not seen her since the day she had left him, aged nine. Her greeting was classic. "Well, who are you then?"

"I'm James Ashworth, Nanny".

"Well, I wouldn't have recognised you".

He divulged that he had born a distinct grudge against the lady whom he had adored and who had seemingly disappeared from his life

Wearing Jeremy's mortar board at his Graduation (1986)

*Kitty Hall's Christening
(Jeremy's daughter – 1993)*

*Mary with Thomas Clark, Alice's son
(1987)*

with no warning or explanation. They were best pals again. Penny and Peter Lapsley drove up from London and Suffolk with their spouses, and my three were there with theirs. Jeremy, the last of the 'babies' was deputed to make the speech which he did with relish, reminding everyone that he hoped they had remembered lessons from nursery days, and, having been properly brought up, would all have washed their hands before tea. The cake was cut, presents given and Nanny, with her hair newly permed, suddenly looked vulnerable in her best polyester dress as her eyes welled up and she thanked everyone between tell tale sniffs.

My present to her was to be a holiday, which, true to form, she was less than enthusiastic about.

"Well, I haven't got anyone to go with".

"Yes, you have Nanny. I'm going to treat you and a friend to a week away and you can choose where that will be, so how about Mrs Stannard?" I knew it was more likely to be Scotland than Africa.

"Oh I don't suppose she'll want to leave her daughter, Angela".

I had not envisaged that my largesse should include more than two people, so I suggested that Mrs Stannard (always referred to thus, even though I knew her name was Florrie) should be invited. She was of course only too delighted at the thought of a free holiday, and accepted with alacrity. Brochures piled up, decisions were deferred and telephone calls between Swaffham and Cromer multiplied. Finally, the decision was made. It was to be a coach trip – "not too far, Mrs Stannard feels sick in buses" to the Yorkshire Dales. Both ladies were ardent fans of 'All Creatures Great and Small' and the itinerary included a visit to the film venue as well as to Haworth Rectory to see the Bronte Museum. But there was a problem. Mrs Stannard had difficulty with stairs so all the various hotels had to be checked out for the existence of either a lift or a downstairs bedroom. I, for my part, hoped that once the said week was over I would never have to hear another word about coach tours to Yorkshire.

"Mrs Stannard thinks it would be best to go when the weather is nice". Fine, except that Yorkshire is not noted for blue skies. June was to be the chosen month.

"Mrs Stannard thinks we should take a picnic for the journey".

Mrs Stannard came to stay at Cley Road for the two days

preceding the 'off' so that there was ample time to prepare the said picnic as well as to discuss what to take and then to pack it. The coach was to leave at a very early hour and I was to deliver them to the coach station.

"In plenty of time please. Mrs Stannard gets worried if she thinks she is going to have to hurry". They were both standing expectantly at the bus station at 5.30am even though the coach was not due to leave until 6.20. A week later I met the coach on its return and greeted two smiling ladies who told me that, "Yes, it was really quite nice. The hotel was a bit near the motorway so we stayed indoors, but we had some nice outings and we saw Robert Hardy filming which was very nice. We didn't think much of the factory visit though".

"Oh, what sort of factory was it?"

"Something to do with cloth I think. There were a lot of machines there".

I duly received a very touching, and probably rather expensive Thank You card from Mrs Stannard, telling me that she and Mary had had a wonderful time chatting and laughing about old times like they used to do when they were both girls at Heacham. And Nanny presented me with an embossed notepad from Haworth which I have had beside the telephone ever since.

She came to work the next day as if nothing had happened. Holiday or no holiday, the brass was tarnished, the litter in the kitchen needed tidying, the airing cupboard looked as if it needed a sort out. How, I mused, would I ever cope without Nanny if a mere week got me into such disarray? It took her no time to restore order.

Retirement was talked about but constantly deferred. Instead it was decided that she would only undertake tasks which she enjoyed. Ironing was well within her scope, as was mending or stitching on nametapes for Alice's children. She came when the weather was nice and when she felt like it, and so for a few more years she kept decrepitude and senility at bay. But bills and paperwork she found beyond her, and everything from junk mail to the telephone bill came my way. At her request, I, who loathe paperwork and anything that arrives in a brown envelope, took power of attorney. As the years advanced and Nanny's memory and mental faculties diminished, she required more and more supervision whilst always reminding me that "I don't want to be a nuisance". She frequently was, but as son Mark put it "It's payback time, Mum". True.

Chapter 11

I had been a widow for five years, a grandmother twice over, and life in Swaffham was happily uneventful until a chance meeting in Woolworths was to change everything. There I encountered our former Vicar from Rockland St Mary who I knew was somewhere in Breckland, but whom I had not seen since he'd left the village two years before. It was Kit Chalcraft, whose wife I was later to become. He looked ill and wretched and I soon learned that he had been dogged by marital problems and was now on his own trying to cope with ten isolated rural parishes. Furthermore he was suffering from glandular fever. With three of his four children abroad, only John, the youngest, now at Caius College, Cambridge, was at home at Gooderstone Rectory from time to time. I immediately invited him back to the house and Nanny, veteran member of Kit's former Mothers Union, was as delighted as I was to see him again. When I told her that his marriage had collapsed and he was on his own she said, "I'm not surprised. Strange lady. He doesn't look well does he? Probably not had a square meal for weeks". Dead right. He had apparently been existing on Paracetamol and boiled eggs. We soon countered that.

It wasn't to be long before Nanny became a valued team member when it became necessary to dodge the press who were soon to be stalking us. I soon discovered that a divorced Vicar, far from being regarded with compassion, is more likely to be shunned by his clerical colleagues. A twice-divorced Vicar is beyond the pale. News of the break-up of his first marriage had been common knowledge when we were all still living in Rockland St Mary. Then he had struggled gamely on alone, coping with his job as well as with teenage son John who was still at school and living with him in the Rectory, and with visits from his ever supportive older children when they returned home from time to time. I remembered Kit's pride when his eldest daughter got a double first in history at Caius College, Cambridge, prompting Nanny to say, "Times must have changed since I was there. They didn't have girls then". The significance of Marianne's degree did not, alas, register.

His last visit to me before leaving the village to take up his new post a couple of years later was memorable. He came to say goodbye and to tell me that he was getting married again to a lady from the next-door village. After expressing my delight and good wishes I remarked that he must now be in a great state of euphoria and hopefully sufficiently in love to be off his food.

"Oh no, it's not like that at my age. I'm just so thankful that anyone wants to marry me at all, and we'll make a good team. I'm hopeless on my own. She's a widow and she likes playing the organ in church which will be a great help as we shall be in very isolated parishes and I don't suppose there are many people wanting to do that".

"So why are you going there and where is it".

"Breckland, in West Norfolk. I'm very lucky to have been given another parochial job because divorced parsons are not what PCC's choose. Actually, when I went to be interviewed I was told that they wanted a married priest, so it's as well that I'll be able to fulfil that". It all sounded less than inspiring and I remember thinking that perhaps our unworldly and certainly un-street-wise Vicar might be falling into a yawning elephant trap. I later learned that all his children had felt the same.

I recounted my conversation to Nanny and knew she'd elaborate on the subject. So what did she think of it all and in particular what did she think of the lady, who I had never met. I knew that the gossip would be top topic at Mothers Union meetings. It was. Nanny's reaction was typical. She just said, "Well... mm..." It was the deprecating sniff that followed that said more than any words could have done.

The lady did not like Breckland, she did not like rural isolation, she did not like the job, she did not like the Chalcraft children and she very soon did not like Kit either. Her ultimatum that either he got himself transferred or she'd be off, resulted in the latter. She returned to her own house from whence she had come forthwith. He acknowledged that he had made a hideous mistake which had devastated him. His self-confidence was in tatters and the isolation afforded him by fellow clergy who were clearly either too embarrassed, or too shocked to proffer some hospitality, didn't help. This was a Vicar who had only ever wanted to be a parish priest in a rural community, who had been loved and revered by his parishioners for whom he had always worked tirelessly, doubtless to the detriment of his own family, but whom he now felt he had let down.

Although Kit had told his churchwardens and parishioners as well as his immediate boss, the suffragen Bishop of Lynn, of our involvement, and of his intention to resign when we married, the diocesan Bishop of Norwich decided to sack him. He had received a letter from a local woman who, as well as having a passion for God, had a daughter who seemed to have one for Kit. She had turned up at the Rectory before breakfast (no doubt hoping to find he was not there, thus adding fuel to her hellfire) to ask Kit if it was true that he was 'having a relationship with a widow.' After hearing his affirmative reply she said that unless he agreed to stay indoors at the Rectory so that he could spend time 'getting it sorted out with God' she felt that she or her mother must write to the Bishop to tell him (as if he didn't already know) This she then did, and gave the letter to Kit to read with the threat that it would be posted if he did not concur with her wishes. He returned it to her, accepting the consequences.

Meanwhile the lady came to see me to persuade me that Kit and I must only ever be platonic friends. Anything else would be wicked. She told me that she had been obliged to visit me after letting her Bible fall open as she always did for guidance. It evidently said something to the effect that she should 'take up her mantle of righteousness.' Uncertain that this was sufficient to prompt her to action, she again let the good book fall from her hands and this time it lay open where a passage decreed that 'in the face of evil, the good must scourge the earth of sinners' or something like it. She told me that she and her daughter had been praying all night for the soul of Kit. Mine seemed not to feature in her ministrations. I suggested that instead of encouraging her daughter, who was in her mid thirties, to such piety, I thought she should be encouraging her to find a nice boyfriend.

She finally left my house after four hours. I don't know if she had found the encounter rewarding. I had found it totally exhausting, and it had done nothing to promote my ever-diminishing good humour. There are some people with whom one can have an enlightening conversation despite fundamental differences. It was not the case with this woman who, on reflection, I concluded was so entrenched in her ludicrous sanctimony that I might as well have been talking to a foreigner with no knowledge of English, let alone common sense.

The furore which followed was something we had never envisaged. The media were hot on our trail. This was a story which could run and run, for the combination of a Vicar and a former television personality was the stuff of scandal. The pity of it was that I was not the wife of the organist, there was no sex orgy in the vestry, nor were there any former spouses crying in the aisles. Nonetheless television crews, most of whom I knew and had worked with in the past, pitched up, together with newspaper reporters, but because I was myself 'media savvy' things went very much our way. Sue Lawley became something of a mentor, advising me who to give interviews to and who to avoid. Valerie Grove from the Times and Elizabeth Grice from the Telegraph were welcomed, and drove up from London before writing extremely sympathetic articles. The lady from Sky and another from The Sun were not.

'Doorstepping' as it is called, is easily avoided, at least it is if you happen to live in a house up a drive and can see approaching cars or visitors. I easily spotted cameras flashing the giveaway red light, which shows that they are running, just as I spotted their crews all advancing towards the house. As the knocker on the front door was thumped, I knew that the cameraman would be poised to catch me as I opened it, so I deliberately stood behind it, invited the accompanying reporter to step inside, and closed the door smartly. The film of the reporter coming in and out of my house was not what they had come for. But when it was BBC or Anglia crews that I knew and trusted, I gave them brief but adequate interviews. Knowing that Kit would be an easy target for any unscrupulous reporter, I asked both cameramen to guard him carefully should they be scheduled to visit him. He told me later that the BBC cameraman, Hank, an old friend and working colleague of mine, had indeed been sent to the Rectory to film a hoped for interview, and on arrival had sidled up to him whispering, "Don't say a word and don't agree to being interviewed. Just say you'll walk up and down the road and I'll film you doing that". It was footage that was shown again and again on various news bulletins.

Nanny became our most valued ally. She it was who fielded telephone calls as I stood beside her, and in her expressionless voice warded off speculative visitors with "I really can't say if Mrs Hall will be here or not. Perhaps you had better ring again. The Reverend Chalcraft? No, he lives at Gooderstone Rectory". She was unphased by the circus that surrounded us and was therefore the perfect foil. Indeed, stressful though it was there was also a lighter side to the whole scenario, and moments that we all positively enjoyed. Listening

Kit and Susanne with her grand-daughter Scarlett, daughter of Alice (1995)

to Nanny playing the dumb cluck when answering the door to suspicious strangers was always entertainment of the first order. I would be despatched as her children had been in years gone past with a "You stay there. I'll see to the door". I didn't argue.

The churchwardens that supported their Vicar were collectively sacked, as were the parochial church councils. What Peter Nott, the poor Bishop of Norwich, did not realise was that by taking such action he had lost the plot. Norfolk village people, be they churchgoers or not, will not be told that those whom they had themselves elected, were sacked. There was mutiny in the pews and a declaration of independence by five of the ten villages. The remaining five were those who were devoid of any leadership, and had been the very parishes that Kit had tried and failed to rejuvenate, reluctantly conceding that they were moribund.

The Bishop wasted no time in appointing his friend, the Archdeacon of Lynn, to look after the Hilborough Group, as the ten villages were known, until a permanent replacement could be found. It was the first of several episcopal blunders. Such were the loyalties of Kit's parishioners to him that they were not going to pack the pews for any substitute. Apart from the worthy lady and her pious daughter who attended every service, there were few others. Yet for Kit's last few services there had been standing room only. "You didn't expect to see my bum on one of your pews, did you Vicar?" asked one distinctly non-churchgoing wag.

A satirical poem did the rounds of Norfolk causing much mirth. It concerned the brilliant duo 'Kit and the Widow' who had offered their services free in aid of the Norfolk Churches Trust annual party. The Bishop, President of the Trust, would have none of it, insisting that they were billed as Christopher and Tony instead. The evening was a sell out. People, aware of the controversy, scrambled for tickets, and the size of the audience necessitated a larger tent than had originally been planned. The cabaret was brilliant.

The strategy had failed lamentably, so papering feverishly over cracks the Bishop soon appointed one of his middle-aged bachelor priests to replace the Archdeacon in Kit's job, whom he would personally install forthwith. It was all to remain a secret for fear of any reprisals, but as the organist had to be included she soon set the jungle drums rather than the organ relaying the news. The church equivalent of a party political whip decreed that every available member of the clergy should be bussed in to Great Cressingham church to attend the evening service and the day approached.

As for the media, they came with outside broadcast units, arc lights and all that's required to produce a few minutes for national news bulletins. They sensed an imminent showdown, and were not disappointed. Letters from the five parishes that had declared their independence, opposing the appointment, had gone unheeded. The die was cast and the Bishop's man would be foisted on them come what may. They decided otherwise and warned that if their objections were ignored then they would collectively stand up at the appropriate moment during the service and hand in a written pledge withdrawing their duties as churchwardens which, despite their supposed dismissal, they had continued to fulfil. As might be supposed, there was no stampede to replace them, so they stood on firm ground. Thus, when the Bishop turned on his heel in the middle of the service when Kit's churchwardens collectively stood to tell him that they did not accept his diktat, his chaplain poked the organist with the episcopal crook, hissing, "play, play!" At that point all the representatives of the five 'rebel' parishes walked out of the church into the arc lights of the television cameras. Yeoman farmer Cyril Lake, veteran churchwarden of Threxton for 50 years, had plenty to say when asked by the BBC's Mike Wooldridge what he thought of his Bishop. "What Bishop? We've just sacked ours for incompetence". His wife Dot, a former wartime landgirl who had minded her church with loving care since marrying Cyril, was asked what she would do if the Bishop locked her out of her church. The reply, in her rich Norfolk dialect was classic. "He couldn't do that. There's only one key and I've got it". What more could any television reporter ask for? It was 'Parish Pump' at its best. Dot Lake hadn't bargained for appearing on national news programmes, and she certainly hadn't expected to be accorded heroine status everywhere she subsequently went to shop in Watton.

The churchwardens and parish council members, undeterred by their airbrushing from the diocesan yearbook and supposed relegation to the wilderness, became ever more gung-ho and decided to employ and pay their own Vicar. And that meant Kit. Except that he demurred. That, for him, was one step too far. Instead, Robert Van de Weyer, author, lecturer and, to authoritarian prelates, maverick priest, took the baton. A brilliant and charismatic preacher with an inherent aversion to dictatorial churchmen, he would be happy to travel from his home in Huntingdon to take services each Sunday. He had never accepted pay for his ministry, so providing him with fuel for his car was well within the financial scope of the parishes as they built up their resources. They called themselves the Oxborough Circuit, withheld the ever increasing sums required for quotas payable to the diocese, working on the theory that as they provided their own priest and cost the diocese nothing, why pay?

It took a year to persuade Kit to resume taking services and when he did so the churches were full and growing fuller. The finances, thanks to a clever and astute chairman, John Davies, were healthy, and the churches themselves were in excellent order. Kit ruefully remarked that he seemed to have ended up with all that a country parson could ever wish for – full churches and the time to look after his parishioners.

In many ways life was stimulating. In other ways it was testing. Kit was still shunned by the majority of his former local colleagues who were either too scared to risk their own livelihoods by associating with him, or perhaps too embarrassed. But there were those that dared to visit him, notably the local Methodist Minister and his former curate, Gordon Wheatley, and letters from others all over the country as well as from lay people arrived by the hundred. Nanny of course remained unmoved by what was going on. She even said as she shook her head in wonderment one day, – "well, like I always say – it's just one of those things".

By nature bookish and unworldly, Kit had been so exposed by the media that he was easily recognised wherever he went, particularly when wearing his dog collar. On one occasion, which caused much amusement, he was outside the bank near the traffic lights in Swaffham getting some money from the hole in the wall, when a truck drove up and ground to a halt as the lights went red. Down went the drivers' window, and a voice called out "Rootin' for yer Vicar. If you'd been 'omo they'd have made you a Bishop by now!"

To everyones' relief we managed to keep the details of our wedding a secret and apart from our children and my two grandchildren, only

Kit's parents, his loyal churchwardens, his organist and a few of our greatest friends, all sworn to secrecy, came. Alice had already voiced her apprehension that Hello magazine would be there. Having been mortified by the publicity surrounding her mother she took some persuading that with luck we'd be able to avoid it on our wedding day. The local undertaker, Derek Gaskin, with whom Kit had worked on numerous occasions, summoned him to his funeral parlour one afternoon to tell him that, as a present to both of us, he planned to transport him to our wedding wherever and whenever it was to be in his biggest and best funeral car. We didn't imagine he'd be keen to take us to the Registry Office where we had to do the civil rite, but rather to the church service which would be for us the real occasion.

"Do you mean you'll be arriving in the hearse?" I asked?

"Well, I didn't really like to ask if that was the idea. It seemed such a generous offer that I didn't think I could question it", came Kit's reply.

Tactful enquiries revealed that it was an eight seater stretch limo and in it there would also be room for Kit's parents, both well into their eighties, for Nanny and for a splendid old lady, Irene Moreton, of whom we are both particularly fond. I was driven to Little Gidding by one of my sons. Anxiously we awaited Kit's arrival. The tiny church, lit entirely by candles, could only hold thirty-six people, which was perfect. Michael Cansdale, Kit's great friend and a former Oxford organ scholar would do the musical honours, not on a magnificent instrument, there being no organ, but on his accordion. Robert Van de Weyer would conduct the service.

Spot on time the funeral cortege swept into the forecourt, plastic flowers adorning the back window, and from it alighted the passengers. Christine, Kit's mother, when asked if she had had a good journey replied, "Splendid. But of course for us oldies it was a bit like a dress rehearsal!" Indeed it was.

Christine died several years later aged 94 and was transported to her funeral, not in the stretch limo but in the hearse, driven on her final journey, as she had been on that happier occasion, by Derek Gaskin.

To my great regret, my own mother did not know Kit. Aged 78, she was still riding sidesaddle as she had done all her life, and hunting regularly. Having bred many racehorses, whose careers she followed, she was particularly fond of one rather flighty youngster, which was in training near where she lived in Herefordshire. Unbeknown to me she drove over to ride it each week. On one fateful day when cantering down a green lane, it took fright at something, probably her flapping side-saddle skirt, bolted to the end where it hit the road and fell, pitching my mother on to the hard tarmac. She never fully recovered before she died eight months later. Although she regained consciousness after several weeks in a coma in intensive care, following an operation in the neurological centre at Smethwick, she was brain damaged. She knew me and she knew my children, but insisted that the grandchildren were also mine, rather than my daughter Alice's. She never laughed again and she never walked, despite all the possible available treatment. But once she was transferred first to Swaffham Hospital and then to a nursing home nearby, I was able to bring her home daily. Convinced that Kit was the man who came to mend the television, we left it at that. She never knew that her only child's second husband was not the chap who fixed the telly.

Chapter 12

But this is Nanny's story rather than mine. To my delight, a ginger feral cat seemed to have taken a shine to her and decided that her house was preferable to the wild life, and appeared every evening for the proffered saucer of milk. Gradually, wild though it clearly was, it timidly crept through the back door, then on to a chair and finally, daringly, on to her lap. She now had a live-in friend and accordingly her conversation was soon dominated by the topic of cats. Her neighbour, Mrs Helson, a chatty octogenarian, was soon briefed to 'mind the cat' during Nanny's absence when working for me, and although I did not realise it at the time, it was I think the defining factor of her slow but steady decline towards the senility that was to so afflict her ten years later. Sadly the cat was no panacea.

Convinced that a smell had invaded her house, she attributed it to the cat. I could smell nothing, neither could Alice or her husband Christopher, or anyone who visited her. Nanny, who had never previously had any sense of smell, gradually became so convinced of its existence that she began to systematically wash everything from all her clothes to the bedclothes, curtains, walls and even carpets. Not just once but repeatedly. The smell, she insisted, was so bad that she must get rid of the cat. The vet who was briefed about the problem did confirm that the cat which was quite old, probably had cancer, but was definitely not responsible for any evil odour which affronted only Nanny. He eventually agreed that as it was ailing anyway and was causing its owner such unaccountable grief, it should be put down. It must have sensed its imminent demise because as soon as I appeared carrying a wire basket, borrowed from the vet, it reverted to its feline habits. It snarled, scratched and clambered round the room in a thoroughly scary fashion. Eventually, clad in coats, hats and gloves as protection against scratching or worse, I managed to plonk the cage over it as it scampered across the table. By this stage ornaments, pictures and anything in its wake had been strewn wildly about. But we had caught it, and so ended the advent of the cat. It was delivered to the vet with the recommendation that the requisite fatal injection might best be administered through the wire. Two years after its arrival it was clear that the phantom smell had been purged, the house no longer needed the constant and obsessive cleaning, the washing machine was not on full load daily, nor the washing line bedecked with blankets and bedspreads. No further mention was made of the cat and even the arrival of Christmas cards bearing pictures of every sort of loveable moggie failed to cause any comment.

Mention of the cards reminds me of the many times that we were to give Christmas lunch to Nanny and Kit's parents, sometimes on the day itself, or the day before if we were joining other family members. All our guests were deaf, all of them shouted at each other, heard very little if anything, and the irritation it caused me never diminished. The unwrapping of presents always took forever and more often than not the gift within the paper was greeted with, "Well, I don't know what I'll do with that I'm sure". Meltis Fruits were Nanny's favourites, and once word got around they came in abundance, resulting in "I do quite like them, of course, but I don't need this many". My son, Mark, remained in the jigsaw mode. She had always enjoyed doing them, he enjoyed buying them for her and remained oblivious to the fact that alas no one seemed to enjoy doing them these days. "I thought I told you last year that I don't do jigsaws any more. I haven't got a table big enough and anyway I can't see like I used to".

She was far more forthright than were the recipients of her gifts of socks. Years ago it had been my husband, Tom, then our sons, then Christopher and finally Kit who were annually presented with three pairs of dark grey socks. They always assured her that they were badly in need of the said socks and agreed with her observation that "Without me to darn the old ones, I expect you need them".

If my children and their families were with us for Christmas there was always much laughter surrounding the undoing of presents. As the small children scrabbled round the tree grabbing parcels as their parents tried to list the donors, the old people sat apart slowly opening one at a time. Kit's mother, receiving a photograph of two of her great grandchildren looked at it for a long time, finally passing it to her husband, Roland, saying, "I don't know who they are. I think it's for you".

Lunch would be planned to finish in time to hear the Queen's speech, through which they usually slept.

2002 was probably the most dire of our Christmases. Kit's father, now aged 95, far from crumbling after the death of his wife, continued to live on his own and to manage well, as he still does today. With the help of a microwave he 'cooks' for himself, spurning the suggestion of having meals delivered to him. With the sports channel of Sky television showing him wall-to-wall coverage of all the events which he's always enjoyed, life was good. It was not so good after he broke his wrist and had to have it in plaster for several weeks. Reluctant to be with other people at mealtimes when he needed his food cut up, we were a fairly dismal foursome on Christmas Day. He was always pleased to see Kit's children and grandchildren whenever they visited us, as well as my son Mark, in whom he found a fellow sports enthusiast. But this year he told us that he didn't feel up to having any of the small children around him, and he certainly wouldn't go anywhere. The conversation at lunch centred entirely on the subject of hearing aids, with Nanny and Roland seemingly delighting in persuading each other, and us, that they didn't work and weren't worth having.

It had taken me months to persuade Nanny that she needed one, (for my sanity as much as her own) and I had duly invested £500 in a hearing aid for her, which had been carefully fitted into her ear, tested, and proved effective. I had not bargained on having to persuade her to wear it. She, after umpteen "I beg your pardons" to everything that was said to her, and my remonstrances that she hadn't got her hearing aid in, would somewhat triumphantly volunteer, "It doesn't work, of course. My sister's never did either". My voice rising, I would hiss, "NO, Nanny, it only works if you switch it on". The next retort would be, "Well, the batteries don't last you know". She had a drawer full of them. Is there some sort of dogged determination in old people not to harness modern technology to their needs? Kit's father, the possessor of an even more up to date and expensive hearing aid, also seems to take some sort of subverse pleasure in declaring it to be "no good, you know. Doesn't work!" Conversations with deaf people can be as exasperating as they can be amusing, and one in particular which I heard is memorable. It concerned carnations and Dalmatians and went as follows.

"I love carnations".

"So do I. The more spots the better".

"Spots? I've never seen spotted ones. Do they smell as good as the others".

"Well, I've never heard of any others. I don't know about the smell".

"D'you have them?"

"No, but I have a friend who bred eight and sold them for a fortune".

When Mrs Helson, Nanny's similarly deaf neighbour, moved into an old people's home, it meant that the only congenial local friend had gone, leaving an empty house beside number 29, Cley Road. On the other side was the proverbial neighbour from hell whose swearing and that of her unruly children could be heard from the street, but luckily not by the lady whose hearing aid 'didn't work.' Then came a garbled account of how the family was having to move, due to some skulduggery involving mail order parcels, and visits from the police. Hardly surprisingly, with an empty house on either side of her, she and I concluded that the moment had probably come to find some sheltered accommodation. Mary Church's name was added to a list of those hoping to gain admission to Hilton Court, an enclave of self-contained flats built round a central courtyard in the centre of the town, overseen by a warden. We were lucky.

Three months later one became available, and with the help of my children we accomplished the move. All Nanny had to do was to push her wheeled tartan shopping trolley to her new abode after spending most of the day in our house. We all accepted that she was now officially 'retired' and far from her resenting that we now had Denise Manning as her replacement, she welcomed it. I had found someone who was as efficient and as good company as Nanny had been, and the two of them soon became friends. It was not long before Denise undertook to 'do' for Nanny, a luxury to which she had never been accustomed, but which she richly deserved. We had had the flat carpeted and fitted with a new electric cooker and fridge. She seemed genuinely delighted. She was much nearer to our house as well as to the centre of the town, and the daily trip to collect her newspaper, followed by a visit to the Co-op ,was even eased by the provision of a press button pedestrian crossing. She never went out without the shopping trolley but I began to have reservations about its safety, having neither brakes nor steering. She, of course, thought it was perfectly adequate and resisted my inclination to change it for a folding wheeled walking frame. Finally,

Just after the move into 15 Hilton Court

the fact that such a thing also had a seat built into it, persuaded her to take to it. From then on Nanny and her crimson walking chariot were inseparable. It fitted into her porch cupboard and it's presence or absence there was my way of telling if she was at home or not. On it she would journey everywhere.

Outside 15 Hilton Court, Swaffham – Sheltered accommodation flat and Mary's last home (2004)

On one of Mary's many visits to our house, pushing her wheeled chariot, mere weeks before she died.

I've often wondered if it was the move which escalated the mental deterioration that had been slowly advancing. Denise and I had many a conversation about the worrying signs of dementia that we both increasingly noticed. When the cold weather arrived, I reminded Nanny to wear her nice thick coat that we had bought together the previous winter in King's Lynn.

"It's not mine. None of the things that are hanging up here are mine. I don't know what's happening but someone has taken all my things and put someone else's in my cupboard".

"No, Nanny, surely you remember our trip to King's Lynn when we bought the coat and then had it made shorter to fit you".

"I hear what you are saying, but I know what I know. Someone is playing tricks on me and putting strange things in my house. It's not my coat. I've never seen it before".

Next came the hiding of things – in particular, money. Every week she collected her pension and seldom spent even half of it. The money accumulated in a wallet in a drawer until I paid it into her bank account from which household bills were paid by banker's orders. She had long since ceased to use her chequebook. To be fair, it had always been something which she regarded with grave suspicion. Years before she had reluctantly agreed to have a bank balance so that I could pay her wages directly into her account, and then years later a pension. But still she preferred to cash a cheque for the amount required by the council or for the electricity bill, and to go to the various offices to pay the bills in person and in cash. When it was the council tax it even meant a bus trip. I gave up suggesting that it would be easier to post a cheque. The familiar response was always, "Oh, but there's no telling that it will get there".

I always checked to see that she never had too much cash in the house lest she was the victim of a thief or a sharp salesman. One such charlatan had already persuaded her to buy an exorbitantly expensive vacuum cleaner that was far too complicated for her ever to use.

It came as a surprise when she arrived at our house one day somewhat breathless to tell me that the warden had asked her if she'd like a ticket for the draw and she couldn't buy one because she had no money.

"Someone has taken it all you know. I'm always telling you that people come when I'm out or else in the night and take away my things". Margaret, the warden, also rang me to say that she was a bit concerned about Mary as she seemed to have lost her money.

I returned with her to Hilton Court and sure enough, the wallet had disappeared, her purse was empty and she was extremely agitated. I rootled in all the drawers and eventually found her money, her wallet and purse and her pension book all hidden amongst her clothes. This became a routine occurrence and I retrieved things from saucepans, from shoes and even from the bathroom medicine chest. Her hearing aid was constantly hidden and whenever I visited her, by now almost daily, the first task was to find it, test it and put it in her ear. And as I did so I would tease her with, "And now Nanny you'll be able to tell me that it doesn't work!" Despite the fact that she frequently exasperated me, we still had great rapport, and reference to the hearing aid would amuse us both. Strangely, her behaviour was not uniform. There would come times when the old Nanny re-emerged and she would tell me that she felt as if she was being overtaken by her failing memory.

"Something's happening" she'd say.

"What, Nanny?"

"I don't know. But it's something I can't quite explain".

She still welcomed the occasional visits from her nephew Tony and his wife Betty, from her niece Joan and her husband Laurie from Bedford, from my children and from their children, but they were rare occurrences and apart from a daily visit from the warden and from either Denise or me, she was clearly lonely. In a vain attempt to get her integrated into the extremely friendly community in which she now lived, I tried to persuade her to accept the invitations of the warden to join her neighbours on coach outings. But no. That determined shake of the head brooked no argument.

"I'll go to the Friday lunches, but you see, I don't think anyone wants to talk to me. They all talk to each other, and anyway I like to keep myself to myself". Nonetheless, she went to a community lunch each Tuesday, as well as the weekly get together on Fridays, organised by the warden, Margaret. The hairdresser came fortnightly and the chiropodist monthly. Everything at Hilton Court was to her liking, except for the shower.

"I can't make it work and I don't like all that water coming at me from up above". For someone who had graduated from a tin bath in the front room to constant hot water coming out of bath taps, the transition to shower was too much. She doggedly refused to use it.

She would occasionally accompany me to join the other occupants of Hilton Court when the sunshine beckoned them out on to the garden seats, but it was I who did the chatting.

"Come on, Nanny. It's a lovely day and there's Rosie sitting out there now with the others. You know her". Out we would both go to an always friendly welcome, but joining in was something that never really happened. Instead she would far prefer to get her wheeled walking frame out of the porch and set off by herself at a steady pace on a daily walk round the town regardless of the weather. On went her woolly hat and her quilted jacket, and as well as weekly sorties to the Post Office to collect her pension, she made frequent peregrinations round the aisles of the Co-op as well as down the aisle of the church. This, she always attended on Sundays, unless she came to services which Kit took. There was no question of her losing her mobility even if her mind was gradually failing her.

When the new Bishop of Norwich took over from his predecessor, Peter Nott, he very soon came to Swaffham to see us and then to take a service at Didlington where he re-licenced Kit. Nanny's classic response as we came out of the church afterwards was, "Well, about time too. I always did think all that how-di-do was silly. But there you are – just one of those things".

Chapter 13

During one of her more lucid periods and during the build up to the second gulf war, Kit and I went to play golf in Portugal. On our return I went straight off to Hilton Court (it took me just under two minutes, door to door on my bike) and asked Nanny how she had been, and had anything happened while we had been away? I found her in very sparky form.

"Yes", she said, "I had a funny telephone call".

Surely she had not been the victim of the heavy breathing brigade?

"What sort of call?", I tentatively enquired.

"Well, it was a gentleman asking me if I had been in the forces and telling me that I would need to be reporting to RAF Marham for the war".

"What?", I expostulated. "Did you have your hearing aid in?"

"Yes, I did and I asked him to repeat it several times".

"So what did he say?"

"First of all he asked if I was Mary Church and I said yes. Then he asked if I had been in the forces, so I said I had been in the WAAF. So he told me that my name was on a reserve list and I would be getting my papers and my kit would be given to me when I reported to Marham".

This was too much.

"So what did you say?"

"Well, I said I thought there must be some mistake, but he said no he didn't think so and he had had to trace me with lots of other people from the council registers as I had moved. Then he asked me if I was prepared to go. So I said NO, and the way I said it meant that he understood. So he asked me why and I said because I am 88".

I subsequently read in the paper that there had been some astonishing errors in recruitment of reserves, with people who had been demobbed years before, and mothers of children being summoned. Their names had remained on obsolete lists. The thought of Balloon Operator Church on her walking frame in the desert of Iraq had all of us, as well as her, in a state of prolonged giggles.

Now that the behavioural pattern was emerging whereby good days gave way to bad ones, good weeks and even months were uneventful, but a noticeable deterioration always followed a good spell. The doctor had prescribed a variety of medicines. Surprisingly, the taking of them seemed to cause no problems. But the gremlins that invaded her privacy, although held at bay, were never dismissed.

"They came in the night and looked at me in bed", she told me one morning.

"You know, the people that come in here when I'm out. Well, they are coming now at night as well".

I knew that my daughter Alice had fetched her the previous day and taken her home for lunch.

"You went out yesterday, Nanny. Did you have a nice time?" I tested her.

"Yes, a strange lady took me to her house. She had two other people in the car with her (two of her teenage children) and I may be wrong, but I felt as if I had been there before. But I don't know who the people were".

The moment had come when we needed more professional help.

Social Services are, in my experience, a labyrinth of confusion. I was shunted from Dereham to Thetford to King's Lynn and round them all again and again. Telephone call followed telephone call and whichever department I was put through to seemed to be the wrong one. Worst of all is being supposedly 'transferred' and then left listening to the continuous ringing at the other end where the room is either deserted, or its occupants are hoping someone else will answer it. They seldom do. How, I would ask myself, do people who are incapacitated and who have no one to root for them, ever get any attention at all? Getting through to any sort of local government department means travelling a route through thick fog, uphill into a head wind. Worst of all is to be told that the lady you have been doggedly tracking for days on end is either off sick or away on holiday. I've always had a deep rooted, and probably totally unjustified aversion to social workers, and my current experience was doing little to change my feelings. Having eventually located the right department, together with the relevant extension number, I realised that my travail had only just begun. Whoever I spoke to was always going to ring me back. They never did.

Finally, I went to King's Lynn, saw the all important lady who in turn located my next target, and at last we were on the conveyor belt that would lead eventually to our goal. Nanny would have to be visited for an assessment and she might then be eligible for a carer to visit her, or for a place in the local day centre once a week. Knowing that the former Swaffham Granary had been beautifully converted into old people's flats and a day centre, I went to see if Mary Church might be welcome there. It was better than I had ever hoped and the lady in charge there gave me some excellent advice as to how to speed up proceedings. Yes, there was space, yes, of course she would be eligible and would be very welcome. But (yes, the buts were there alright) although the system was complicated, it was navigable and there were short cuts if only they could be found. One of them was to get the doctor on the case, pushing for attention to be given to her patient who definitely needed extra support, and as soon as possible. Nanny's doctor, Grace Barlow, was particularly helpful and, despite being burdened with daily avalanches of paper in our bureaucracy driven world, duly did the necessary.

Weeks later, thanks to endless interference from me, an appointment for the assessment was made. At the appointed hour a man arrived at Hilton Court armed with the inevitable bumph that would baffle anyone, let alone those suffering from dementia. There were of course a great many questions to be answered and forms to be filled in. Had I not been there to translate some of the gobbledygook that was forthcoming, and to fill in all the details, our quest might have failed. 'Which ethnic minority does the applicant belong to?' for instance. Could she dress herself, how far could she walk unaccompanied?

Following the assessment, Nanny was allocated a social worker in King's Lynn who would henceforth be in overall charge of things and with whom I would be required to communicate in future. Mary Church's name finally went up, not exactly in lights, but on the blackboard at the Granary as being a visitor every Tuesday. While there she could have a bath, a hairdo if she so wished, and of course lunch, followed by some sort of collective activity which predictably she wouldn't join in. A carer was assigned to call on her each morning to see that she got dressed and had something to eat and drink for breakfast, and again in the evening to oversee the going to bed routine. Unfortunately the time of the visits varied to such an extent that she was usually up and dressed before the lady arrived, and probably in bed asleep when she returned at night. Nonetheless, she was appreciative of the extra attention afforded her and always recounted to me that it was nice of this strange lady to visit her so regularly. Each Tuesday a minibus called for her, as well as for other people who attended the Day Centre, and a good time seemed to be had by all. If one can overcome the entanglement of paperwork that seems to stifle Social Services, one begins to realise the extent of help available to those who need it. But I remain sceptical as to how it is run, seemingly overburdened by its army of personnel in questionable jobs, three or four of whom it was always necessary to get past on the telephone before hitting the target area.

A call to me from Nanny's niece was worrying. She had had a letter from her aunt Mary in almost illegible script, saying that she was worried by the disappearance of all her money, and the visitations that she was receiving from strange people in the night, who were stealing all her possessions. I began to worry that her troubled mind might now be confusing me with the mythical intruder. The human thought process is such a strange and complex thing that seems to wreak havoc on those who lose control of it, and equal havoc on those surrrounding them. It was no use arguing that there were no alien visitors intent on stealing possessions. Who would want to raid the house of an octogenarian who had never accumulated material wealth anyway? She knew best, and aliens there were. My visits became more frequent and I sped down the road to her on my bicycle two or three times a day. I had taken to checking out her fridge and found, as I had feared, that there was seldom much in it, so each day I put lunch in the microwave for her with explicit instructions writ large beside it as to how to work it, and for how long. It worked well, and perusing the shelves of the Co-op for ready-made meals added a new dimension to her life, and became her new daily task. But not for long. I found her at the till in the Co-op one day clearly confused as to what she had bought, and how to pay for it. There was a 2-litre bottle of milk, a vast packet of cornflakes and tubs of custard. From then on I did her shopping. As I walked her home she seemed strangely silent. "I do seem to be a nuisance now, don't I? And I had some rather bad news yesterday. Mrs Stannard died, and she was the only real friend I still had from my childhood, and it all came back to me. I shall miss her".

Mrs Stannard, who had suffered from osteoporosis, had lived in sheltered accommodation in Cromer, near where Alice's children were at school, and many a time either she or I had transported Nanny to stay with her friend. Whenever her telephone bill arrived, the only calls ever listed were to Mrs Stannard in Cromer. Her death would be a sad loss and had probably accounted for her strange behaviour in the Co-op. Although I had seen Nanny tearful, and in need of the Kleenex, I had never seen her actually overcome. Even then she was persuading me that "I shall soon be alright again, but it's just been a bit of a shock. I'm sorry to burden you with it. I really don't know what I'd do without you". She seemed so crumpled that I too needed the Kleenex, and we both needed a cup of coffee.

To my dismay, Nanny no longer ever watched television. "They don't seem to have proper programmes any more", she'd say every time I switched it on for her, knowing that in all probability she would switch it off as soon as I had left. My suggestions that she should visit us were now greeted with, "But I don't know where you live". But she did still come and frequently at that – presumably on automatic pilot.

Jeremy, the favourite of all her charges, for no better reason than that he had been the baby of them all, came to stay and spent time with his much loved Nanny. She had taken a particular delight in the fact that he and Georgie, his wife, had three appealing children, but now, although she recognised Jeremy, she was unable to put him into the context of his family. No matter. He intended to indulge her. For some time she had frequented the local library, just round the corner from where she lived, borrowing and avidly reading the large type novels that they stocked. If she took out books which she had already recently read it was of no consequence. She never remembered having done so and enjoyed them all over again. As her short-term memory increasingly failed her, so she would forget even the page that she had just read, and start from the beginning again. Jeremy, unaware of the extent of her impaired faculties, decided that talking books would be ideal, and so bought a radio, which played tapes and CD's. He then took her to the library to choose those which she would like to listen to. They came away with several with which he felt she was delighted. As I knew would be the case and had warned Jeremy, they never reached the new gadget. Days later after he had left she remarked to me, "I don't know what that thing is on the table over there. I think someone brought it during the night like all the other things that keep appearing". I returned the tapes to the library and weeks later I returned the radio, still in its virginal condition, to Jeremy.

Chapter 14

Things were getting worse and the horror of having to find residential care loomed. The doctor advised me that it was better to research local homes well in advance of requirements, and I duly concurred. Available space in congenial places were few and far between, and several establishments had recently closed or were about to do so. The first two that I visited were utterly depressing. Old people sat in chairs round the so-called Day Room, their glazed and vacant eyes fixed on the television screen which seemed to be transmitting programmes, either about the DIY skills required to transform houses into modernised and sanitised dwellings, or how to erect and paint decking for the garden. When I attempted to engage anyone in conversation, I was rewarded with blank looks from eyes which somewhat grudgingly abandoned telly-viewing mode to talk to this annoying lady, who seemed to be interrupting things. The smell of urine was all pervading. The horror of old age and all its attendant manifestations reawakened my dread of it.

My last visit was to a home in Swaffham where there was an altogether different atmosphere, not to mention smell. There was an aura of bustling and welcoming staff, those who lived there seemed happy and well cared for and yes, there was likely to be a room available in the not too distant future. That, I presumed, was because one of its occupants was expected to be departing this life fairly shortly. Mary Church's name was duly inscribed on the list of those hoping to gain admission. My next task was to persuade her that it might be nice to live somewhere where she would never be lonely, and would be constantly looked after. Her usual mantra was forthcoming.

"Of course I don't want to be a nuisance, but it would be quite nice to be somewhere where people don't come and take my things". Meanwhile the daily attendance of the carer continued, as did my visits. Denise made sure that the flat was spotless, and the obligatory cup of coffee and a chat became the norm. A very good relationship had developed between them for which I was thankful. Nanny trusted Denise and was always pleased to see her, thoroughly appreciating all that she did, including all her laundry. But both of us knew that the situation was rapidly becoming untenable. It might not be long before she'd have difficulty with her whereabouts.

It was at 8 o'clock one Sunday morning that the telephone rang with the agitated voice of the carer telling me that there was no sign of Mary Church. She seemed to have disappeared. I dressed quickly and was at Hilton Court on my bike within minutes. Nanny had recently said to both Denise and to me that she had had long enough in this world and was ready to go. She hoped to die soon.

"I'd like to think that I shall find my mother when I'm gone" was her spoken wish. My initial fear was that she might have gone off to look for her in this world, namely Swaffham, until I remembered that she had also said that she thought she would go to church on Sunday, even if the weather was bad. It was November. Thus my first port of call was the church. There she was, standing outside with her walking frame, on a bitterly cold morning waiting for the service to begin.

"Nanny, you're too early. The church is shut and the service is not until 10 o'clock".

"Well, never mind. I'll just stand here until I can go in".

I persuaded her to come home for some breakfast, before realising that she was far from well. She spent the day in bed and slept for most of it. The following morning she was no better and was complaining of chest pains. There were no protestations when I called the doctor. As is always the case, the locum doctor was run off her feet and could not be with us until midday. She immediately diagnosed bronchial pneumonia and called an ambulance to take the patient to hospital. I went in the ambulance with Nanny and duly arrived at the Queen Elizabeth Hospital. There we were told that as there were no beds available we would have to stay in the ambulance until space could be found. From there Nanny was loaded on to a trolley and wheeled into the corridor of the Accident and Emergency Department where we remained for seven hours, queuing up for attention with all the other unfortunate victims of accidents or sudden sickness. No wonder that Mr Blair had recently been savagely accosted when he visited the hospital, first by a dissatisfied patient and then by a consultant. Nanny, staunchly conservative, didn't think much to him either.

The rows of people on trolleys waiting to be assessed by a frantically overworked doctor seemed reminiscent of casualties queuing up in hospitals after some unexpected train accident. And this was supposedly Cool Britannia in 2003. In our immediate vicinity was a severely disabled and mentally incapacitated young man lying groaning in the foetal position, while his carer tried vainly to get him attended to. There was an elderly man whose anxious wife was convinced he had had a heart attack.

When the name 'Mary Church' was finally called and she was wheeled into a cubicle it was only to be minutes before she was referred to the X-ray department for the heart attack that she had apparently suffered while waiting immobile on the trolley. Another two hours' wait followed before the X-ray revealed the extent of the damage. But still there were no beds. At 9.30pm she was wheeled into the so-called 'Assessment Ward' to spend the night – a euphemism for the 'when there's nowhere else to go Ward.' Appalled that she was to spend a night on a trolley I asked that she be transferred to the BUPA Sandringham private wing, for which I was quite prepared to pay. The nurse had confirmed that there were available beds there, but returned to tell me that they would not accept her.

"Why not?"

"Because she is too ill and they do not have adequate night cover".

"Are you telling me that you have to be well to go into the Sandringham?"

"Well, it is for patients recovering from operations which have been done there, or for people who have been booked in and assessed".

Exhausted (what on earth could Nanny have been?) I rang Kit to come and fetch me. After spending a comfortable night in a comfortable bed I returned to the dreadful hospital to look for the little old lady who'd started off with pneumonia but had subsequently had a heart attack. A bed had at last been found for her in the morning. There she was in a vast ward, huddled in bed with untouched breakfast, cold and congealed in front of her. She looked hopelessly confused, had no idea where she was and was patently very relieved to see me. All I could think of was how to get her out of what appeared to be a horror place. It seemed to have gone rapidly downhill since my daughter, Alice, spent several weeks in the same hospital before the premature birth of her baby, Jamie. That was ten years ago and she had been well cared for. Now, because of the dreaded MRSA disease, notices proliferated warning everyone to wash their hands – wards were closed because of a prevalent virus, and visitors were barred from others. The nurses, well meaning as they were, were in short supply, clearly run off their feet. Many of them appeared to be foreign. Various items from the Today programme sprang to mind. Had I not heard the Health Secretary, John Reid, telling John Humphreys that due to a massive recruitment drive there were now plenty of nurses in our hospitals? And had he not been asked why so many of them were being imported from such far away places as the Philippines? I concluded that if all the Health supremo did was to rob Peter to pay Paul, depriving poorer countries of nurses and doctors in order to fill our supposedly superior National Health Service, then something was gravely wrong. I have since been told by a consultant that there are more administrators in the NHS than there are doctors and nurses, and in his opinion much of it is now in a state of meltdown, despite the Government policy of throwing ever larger sums of money at it, whilst boasting about hitting their targets. Not exactly cheering news.

There were people moaning and even shouting in this vast mixed ward, which stretched as far as the eye could see. A staff nurse that I managed to corner informed me that the doctors would be round shortly, but that Mary Church would definitely be staying for some considerable time. It was likely to be three weeks, and as there was such a shortage of staff, I deduced that it would probably be spent slumped in a chair beside her bed.

Realising that if that was to be the case there was little chance of her ever being able to walk again, I took the walking frame in and every afternoon heaved her onto it and pushed her, as she pushed it, down the ward and back. We must have made a comic sight like a somewhat weird version of the Hokey Cokey. By now it was December and the Christmas decorations were adorning the ward. The tree at the far end became our daily goal, and we got a cheery hallo from several beds as we passed. The hearing aid, which had been playing up badly, finally collapsed, and as a result Nanny could not communicate with doctors, nurses, or me. Nor could she communicate with her nephew and his wife, Tony and Betty, who came from nearby Terrington St Peter to visit her.

"Don't worry", said the staff nurse "Just go down to the Audio Department on the floor below and they will be able to fix it".

This meant another long wait in a queue, but by now being well conditioned to the system I had a book with me. It was my turn at last.

"I think this hearing aid needs new batteries and a test to see if it is working", I volunteered.

"Is it an NHS model? If not, I'm afraid we don't touch them".

I took it home instead and Kit duly fixed it. The following day Nanny had an operational hearing aid again and was greatly relieved to be able to know what was going on around her. Her Christmas cards surrounded her bed and a photograph sent by the Lapsleys was constantly perused. Despite the labelling she had no idea who any of the people featured in it were, but enjoyed being told over and over by me that it was Penny and Peter, who she had looked after when they were children, together with their families. In fact when Penny's two babies had been born, Nanny had gone to look after each of them for a month. Now they were grown up.

"Oh, really? Well I wouldn't have recognised them. Who did you say they are?"

Knowing that we had a superb cottage hospital in Swaffham, I resolved to get a transfer if I possibly could. More battling with bureaucracy. More exasperation. The nurses at the Queen Elizabeth did a sterling job on the telephone trying to clear a way for a bed to be allocated at Swaffham. Similarly, one of the nurses there who had looked after my mother all those years ago did her best to make it possible. It was the nurses, rather than the army of official personnel in the Department of Social Services, who proved the more effective which makes one wonder if all the mountain of form filling and the bureaucracy, about which I had become increasingly aware, is indeed just propping up an ever increasing number of disposable jobs. Redistribution of personnel from the blunt ends of telephones into the wards would surely not come amiss.

When Nanny was finally allowed to leave King's Lynn for the friendly and welcoming Cottage Hospital, I felt a surge of relief. She would be there just in time for Christmas, she could come out daily and gradually she would be able to regain her strength and, I hoped, return home. It is a hospital where even being ill could be tolerable and Nanny was under the happy delusion that she was staying in a hotel. I didn't disillusion her. Her nephew and niece, Tony and Joan, were similarly relieved, not to say surprised that we had successfully engineered the transfer.

Christmas Day was memorable for all the wrong reasons. Kit's father, now nearly 97, had no intention of going anywhere. With his usual impeccable manners he did accept our invitation to lunch, but not with any degree of enthusiasm. His world had shrunk but he had the huge advantage of retaining all his mental faculties. Kit was and still is kept abreast of every sporting triumph that he will have watched, and that includes cricket and rugger matches round the globe and golf tournaments from all the great venues. An accomplished sportsman in his youth, his interest has never waned and, thanks to Sky television, serves him well in his dotage. Nanny, though a decade younger, had suffered from the ravages of her diminishing mental health, and although she was pleased to come out to lunch, it was an effort for her. The transportation, one by one, of very old people who find getting into a car difficult and getting out of it more so, takes far longer than one ever allows. The hats, coats, mufflers, gloves, walking sticks all have to be dealt with before the shuffling into the drawing room to the fire and the undoing of presents. These seem to take for ever to unwrap and seldom produce more than a "Well, I'm not sure what I'll do with that". There is a limit to how many chocolates old people can eat.

Yes, Christmas was a re-run of last year with the same conversations about hearing aids, the same attention (lack of) to the Queen and probably a distinct feeling of relief from our guests when they were safely back to base, Roland to his own infinitely superior television set and Nanny to the Swaffham Cottage Hospital, the 'hotel' where she was so beautifully looked after. By the time grandchildren arrived later both Kit and I were exhausted. The year was drawing to its close with a rather sad awareness that there would not be many more similar Christmases, if any.

Chapter 15

Three weeks later I took Nanny back to her flat under the supervision of various carers who this time, instead of coming each morning and evening, would call three times a day. She had been well enough to come out each day and had even been out to lunch with Alice. But she was frail. Her carers left notes telling me what time they had called and how they had found Nanny, and I wrote notes back. I asked them to make sure that she took the various pills that had been prescribed. "Oh, I am afraid that is not allowed. It's against the rules to administer drugs".

"But surely the alternative is that someone with dementia might swallow the lot, or else not take them at all. Does that mean that if I'm not here, she will have to go without them even though you're here?"

"Yes, I'm afraid so. That's the regulations. Silly, I know. But if you would get the tablets out of the bottle and put them somewhere safe, then when I come in I will offer them to her".

I did. I also came round to see that she swallowed them, as did Denise on the days that she went in.

As I was leaving one day, the electric light bulb blew in the hall. I called out to the carer who had just arrived, "There's a spare bulb in the middle drawer – could you put it in, please?"

"Oh no. That's against regulations. We are not allowed to do that".

"Are you telling me that if you came in here and found Mary in bed in the dark because her bedside lamp bulb had gone, you'd do nothing even if there was a spare bulb there".

"Yes, I'm afraid so. There's regulations you see".

Social Services and political correctness be buggered, I thought, as I took off my coat and changed the bulb. The Nanny State would rather have this Nanny fall over in the dark and fracture her hip and then clog up a hospital bed than allow a young agile carer to change a light bulb. And all because we have become such a litigious nation that the fear of being sued overrides all else. How changing a bulb could result in learned counsel battling for damages in the High Court escapes me.

As we waited for a room in the care home to become available, I took Nanny to visit it and to my relief she clearly liked what she saw.

"Yes, I think the moment has come. It'll be quite nice to be there". Praise indeed. Meanwhile she gradually resumed her daily saunters round the town, albeit going at a far slower pace. She still delivered all her paperwork to me including the increasing amount of unsolicited and unwelcome junk mail that was plonked through her letterbox on its way to our wheelybin. The waste of money targeting us all, let alone octogenarians suffering from senility is appalling. Why would they need plastic credit cards, be they gold or platinum, to facilitate greater borrowing, when they have long since ceased to remember the existence of their bank account. Offers for bargains at supermarkets mean nothing to someone who shops only occasionally, and then for meagre essentials from the nearest shop. Could someone please form a society for the prevention of such waste? Why not one of the ever increasing governmental departments which seem to be burgeoning as I write?

When we wanted the tree surgeon to cut back branches of a vast beech tree in our garden so as to let the light in to the shrubs and smaller trees, I had to communicate first with a tree surgeon, then with the Tree Officer of the Breckland District Council, followed by the Assistant Tree Officer. Verbose letters explaining all that I could or could not do (if knowledge of trees is on a par with that of grammar in the said department, it did not bode well) came in profusion. No, we may not cut down a self-seeded sycamore that was growing into a wall – didn't we know that all trees in this area had a tree preservation order on them? The dead branch, which hung precipitously from our weeping ash, must be further inspected. If those officers could deal with and curtail the mountain of paper which is delivered daily, they'd be doing more trees more favours than they will ever do in their present job specifications.

The carers who came to see and help Nanny were kind in the extreme. None of them were medically qualified, but dispensed much comfort. The only problem was that their timing continued to vary enormously due to the large round that they had to undertake every day. They might arrive at eight o'clock in the morning, ready to put the kettle on for a cup of tea while supervising the getting dressed. Equally they might turn up at 10 only to exclaim "Well, I never did Mary. You are all dressed up and had your breakfast". The fact that she had put her vest on top of her blouse and was sitting in her hat and overcoat probably passed them by. But their kindliness deserved my admiration. They listened patiently to accounts of how strangers had been in during the night, and they would then leave me a note that 'Mary seemed very confused this morning.' She was also losing a great deal of weight and her appetite had become that of a sparrow. Her photographs, including the one sent at Christmas by the Lapsleys, continued to give her great pleasure and both Denise and I continued to be shown it, usually with the added rider, "of course I don't know who they are".

Dementia, I believe, may in some instances be considerably more distressing for the bystanders than it is for the sufferers. Nanny, as her mind deteriorated, seemed altogether calmer for most of the time. But when the agitation returned she could be extremely aggressive in her insistence that fanciful things were happening to her. If one attempted to contradict her she became even more insistent. On those occasions I usually snapped in irritation, and bid a hasty retreat on my bike. Then, guilt-ridden, I would return soon after to find her all sweetness and light with no recollection of the previous altercation.

Kit and I were to go to Wiltshire in January to spend the weekend with one of my sons in order for Kit to take a service in the local village church. Mark, who had been coerced by his landlady (for whom he had a healthy respect) would be playing the organ. It would be the first time that we had been away since Nanny had been home from hospital. Denise was on standby to visit her in my absence and the carers were alerted. But on Thursday, the day before we were to go, she was far from well again. I rang the doctor forthwith and she came round at lunchtime. Although she could discern a mild chest infection, she seemed extremely reassuring. On hearing that I was anxious about being away, she recommended that, as there was a bed available at the Swaffham Cottage Hospital, Nanny should return there and be supervised. I was assured that there'd be no question of sending her back to the horrors of the Queen Elizabeth Hospital. I took her there, with her walking frame and left her 'back at the Hotel' where she had been so happy previously. The following morning I visited her, took a spare set of clothes as requested by the nurse in charge, and left the number of my mobile phone. We set off for Wiltshire after lunch.

Several hours later as we were nearing our destination the telephone rang. It was the nurse to say that Mary Church was in an ambulance on her way to the Queen Elizabeth Hospital. She had developed a clot of blood in her leg, which was causing concern and could not be treated in Swaffham.

All that I had dreaded seemed to have come to pass and we were a good three hours from home. She was alone and probably on another of those cursed trolleys in the Accident and Emergency corridor in King's Lynn. There was nothing that we could do beyond continue with our journey.

A further telephone call came from the duty surgeon asking for my permission as next of kin to operate on Mary Church.

"I've spoken to the lady but she seemed confused. I told her that due to her age of 89 it wouldn't be advisable to give her a general anaesthetic and therefore would she be happy for the operation to take place under a local one?"

"What did she say?"

"She said Yes".

"Are you telling me that you're going to take her into the operating theatre and cut her leg open while she is fully conscious?"

"Yes, but it's all been explained to the patient and she seems agreeable to everything that we suggested. We just need your opinion and consent".

"Well, I don't give it. For one thing she won't have understood what on earth you were suggesting, and being very deaf she probably didn't hear it anyway. How can you possibly think of operating on a frail old lady who has only just recovered from a heart attack, is very weak and increasingly confused?"

"So what do you think would be the best thing".

"I think that she should be made as comfortable as possible, given something to ease any pain that she may be suffering, and definitely not mauled around with cutting open her leg while she is conscious and won't have the first clue what is happening. It would be absolutely terrifying".

"Her condition is deteriorating and she may not survive if we don't operate. I think she may have been distressed by the journey and then the assessment in A&E".

"Well, if she's so poorly surely the operation will kill her?"

"Yes, of course that's the risk that we'd be taking".

"Well, please don't even consider it. She's already told me several times that she'd like to die now, and it seems rather cruel to try to prevent that if it is likely that the operation itself will kill her".

"I'll have to consult with my superior".

Evidently he did, because mercy of mercies, the superior then telephoned to say that the doctors had decided not to operate anyway, as her condition was now critical and she was not fit to undergo any surgery.

It has always seemed to me that there is a thin dividing line in the rapidly advancing world of medicine between saving life, and actually impeding a dying person from doing so. And if one is unlucky enough to be in a hospital when death approaches, perish the thought of being in the hands of a zealous young doctor, who puts survival of a patient above all else, no matter that he or she might be terminally ill, hoping for peace and pain relief, rather than a few extra torturous days. Dr Shipman's legacy may well prove to be as heinous to people today, as his treatment of his own patients was in the past. Since that ghastly case, what doctor is ever again going to risk upping the morphia, for anyone pleading to be relieved of pain, if it might incriminate him or her?

We were nearing the end of our journey when I rang my son, who in turn managed to locate his sister, who got to the hospital in time to spend the evening at the bedside of the old lady. It was Nanny who had spent so much time with Alice at the beginning of my baby daughter's life. It was Alice, now herself a mother of three who shared Nanny's last evening in this world, and only left her at midnight to return to her own children. Mary Church, precious to all of us, died alas, alone, in the early hours of the morning, as a nurse on the ward informed me on my mobile telephone. There was no one to whom I could speak to find out where Nanny was or what I must do. The only information I could glean was that I needed to go to the special department that deals with deaths, and that would not be possible until Monday.

We drove home on Sunday only to find that the Queen Elizabeth Hospital is indeed in something resembling closedown mode at weekends, so Monday it would have to be.

Once again I went through the main entrance of the most unprepossessing of hospitals to the familiar scene of the A&E, clogged with trolleys stretching down the corridor. But this time I was heading in a different direction towards a waiting room, where three other sombre souls were sitting patiently. We were surrounded by an assortment of carrier bags, all of which clearly contained the possessions of the deceased. I could see the familiar navy blue handbag and shoes of Mary Church atop what was presumably the bag containing her things. Her walking chariot was parked against the wall. I found the whole procedure acutely distressing and was hopelessly tearful. There is something particularly poignant about finding a cherished human being reduced to a few carrier bags. I was given the cheering news that I could not get a death certificate or make arrangements for the undertaker to collect her until a blood relative had signed the necessary form.

"The body cannot be released until we have the signature of a blood relative", said the extremely polite lady from behind her desk, when it was my turn to get her attention.

"But she had no blood relatives".

"Oh it doesn't matter how distant a relative might be, but it must be a blood relative". I was not one.

Increasingly tearful and in no mood for arguing with this particular lady who, like so many others, probably had 'regulations' tattooed on her back, I stumbled from the loathsome room and went instead to the King's Lynn Registry Office, assuming correctly that it was there that I would be able to register the death of Mary Church, no matter what hospital regulations decreed. I was right, but another appointment was required, and another queue to join before I could make it. At least there was one available in the afternoon, and the two hours that I had to kill were happily spent visiting a splendid exhibition in the nearby St Margaret's Church. Later, back at the Registry Office, housed in one of the most beautiful of the old town houses, a thoroughly sensible and sympathetic man understood my plight, and duly signed the necessary paperwork. Armed with this, I returned to the hospital. The body and belongings of Mary Church were released, and she returned for the last time to Swaffham to the undertaker Derek Gaskin's funeral parlour. The second of the wedding passengers in the funeral car had need of his skills, but once again it was not those of a chauffeur.

Knowing that Heacham was to be her final destination, Kit and I went to visit the Vicar there, to ask if it would be possible for the funeral service of Mary Church, and the burial of her ashes after the cremation, to take place there later, and for Kit to officiate at both. Yes, yes, yes said Canon Patrick Foreman to everything. Oh, what a pleasure it was to tell him about the extraordinary lady in question, and to hear him telling us that there would still be some of her contemporaries in the village who he would suggest might attend. He was quite happy for us to 'borrow' his church and no, thank you for suggesting it, but he would be pleased to have someone else take the service, and rather than taking part in it too, have a break. There was something wonderfully refreshing to find a Vicar who did not guard his church jealously, resenting the intrusion of what some others might see as a threat. What we had expected might be a tricky encounter turned out to be a pleasure. After coffee and biscuits with Mrs Vicar in the Vicarage, where we looked out of the window across the garden to one of Norfolk's many magnificent medieval churches, we were taken on an escorted tour. There was the marble memorial to Pocahontas, high on the wall above a much older one to her husband John Rolfe, and on the steps of the nave the instruments and loudspeaker system of an orchestra that would be performing later. This was a church that was clearly still as vibrant as it had been all those years ago. Thus we were only too ready to bolster the coffers by proffering a donation, and we also resolved to attend one of the Lent lunches scheduled to take place on the day in the following month that we planned to bury the ashes.

I was anxious that the service for Nanny should have input from all those who knew and loved her, so emails went out to all her former charges, as well as to the extended family of her foster sister, long since gone, but buried at Heacham. With their consent, her ashes would be buried in the plot containing her foster parents, William and Sarah Gotsell, as well as the ashes of their daughter Ada, and her husband Cecil Flint. That had been her wish and it was to be easily fulfilled. The family would all be attending the service, but would prefer not to take part. Jeremy asked to do her eulogy, and Peter Lapsley, the first of her charges and therefore the oldest, and Scarlett Clark, Alice's fourteen year old daughter, would do the readings, both of which were carefully chosen for the occasion. We knew that the congregation would be small but that would not detract from what we were determined would be the sort of send-off that Nanny would never have dreamed would be hers, but which would be fitting for someone as special as her.

Her will, as well as stating that she wished to be taken back to Heacham, left legacies to both the Children's Society and Barnado's, to my three children, and all else to her nephew and niece Joan and Tony. As is so often the case with people who have been brought up in frugal circumstances, she was always a saver rather than a spender, who could never get used to the idea that she could afford a few luxuries. She had a healthy bank balance, as well as a nest egg invested in a Bank Bond when she died. She had been careful to see that there were always the funds available for the proverbial rainy day, as well as for 'when anything happens to me.' But latterly she had become careless about money. Her pension, if it had not been hidden, would be left lying on her sideboard for all to see. There was always a substantial weekly surplus gradually accruing, which I always insisted on banking, explaining that it was not at all a good idea for her to have large amounts of cash in the house. It's easy to see how vulnerable old people can be to predatory thieves who knock on their doors and then, seeing an opportunity, grab it. Posing as a window cleaner, meter reader or salesman, any opportunist would have had an easy target in Mary Church. Happily she was spared.

Clearing out her flat was a particularly sad task, but with Kit and Denise to help it was soon done. We found birthday cards, one of which was labelled 'Now you are 8', presumably for one of her children's children, perhaps Jeremy's Kitty. In one drawer were colouring books and small toys, waiting for any young visitors. Knitting patterns for every sort of baby garment were carefully stored in a cardboard box, as were a few old photographs of those who had featured in past years, together with the yellowed letters, which had so painfully failed to reveal her identity. There was a bundle of postcards from Peter Lapsley from his first term at prep school saying how much he missed her. And there was a collection of holiday postcards from various Halls, sent to her from skiing resorts, from Cornwall, Australia and Canada. There was a case full of presents that she had been given over the years, still in their wrappers unused, and in her cupboards and drawers and bedside table, tidily folded clothes, her clock, her library card and her Bible and prayer book. Shoes and slippers, well worn, were in the bottom of the cupboard. She had never been one for anything but the 'sensible' variety of shoe, and the style had never changed. Size 4 either laced or buckled and flat heeled in navy blue or black. I found these particularly poignant, as I did her glasses, which had been returned by the hospital. After an operation, which had taken place several years ago to remove the cataracts from her eyes, Nanny had treated herself to some rather jaunty specs. The choosing of these had been much discussed and the ones she favoured resembled, in shape at least, the fly away variety favoured by Dame Edna Everidge. True, they were less flamboyant but we teased her nonetheless, and seeing them other than on her nose, or parked beside her bed, was a painful reminder of the finality of it all. She had always taken such care of them.

We piled everything into dustbin liners and delivered them to the Children's Society charity shop. The glasses went into the recycling box with umpteen other pairs of old specs. She'd have approved of that. No one wanted any of the furniture, minimal as it was, so the van from the house clearance took all but a few souvenirs which I felt should be reminders to my children and grandchildren. Various ornaments went to her niece. Collections of knitting and sewing things, including nametapes of my children and their children went to Alice. Two wartime medals, never worn even on Armistice Day, but still carefully wrapped in the original box in which they had been posted to her at RAF St Faiths in 1945, were to go to Stephen. He, the adopted coloured son of her nephew Tony and his wife Betty told me that he'd always felt an affinity with his great aunt. She had told him how lucky they both were, having been Barnado's children who had finished up with good parents in happy homes. The walking frame went back to Swaffham Cottage Hospital where it will surely have some future use. And so 15, Hilton Court was as empty as when we had first found it. We left the carpets and curtains for the incoming lady and subsequently heard from the warden, Margaret, that she loved the flat and was very happy there. The collection to which all the other residents had subscribed in aid of The Children's Society, in memory of their neighbour who 'kept herself to herself', came to £50. A touching gesture.

Monday February 16th 2004 dawned bright and sunny. Kit always claims that it is a bonus to be able to hold a funeral in good weather, it being far more wretched for the mourners as well as the funeral directors to cope with biting winds or pouring rain. Jeremy and Georgie and their three children had arrived to stay the previous evening, as had Mark. On their behalf as well as my own I made wreaths to go on the coffin. There were aconites and snowdrops in profusion in the garden, which, added to pinks and jonquils from Swaffham's Saturday market, made up into the prettiest of floral cushions. Somewhat averse to the more flamboyant varieties, which so often have white chrysanthemums spelling out the name of the loved one, I opted for the understated. It was so much more in keeping with the lady in question.

We drove to Heacham to find that the hearse was already there, empty. Mary Church was, as I had requested, already in the church waiting for us all to arrive. Not for her the usual maudlin procession of followers after the coffin to the accompanying voice of the parson chanting the familiar verses about resurrection.

I had brought with me a huge cardboard sheet on which I had stuck enlarged photographs of Nanny, from childhood to the present time, which I had gleaned from all sources. It was positioned at the back of the church on an easel for all (and we had grave reservations that there would be no more than a handful) to see. How wrong we were.

To our delight as well as surprise, rather than the sparse collection of mourners that we had anticipated, there were about forty in the church, including several elderly village people who were fascinated with the montage of photographs, particularly as they included school groups dating back to 1920 in which either they or people that they had known featured.

We sang 'The Lord's My Shepherd' and 'Abide with me, fast falls the eventide' which are somehow synonymous with funerals of those of Mary Church's generation, and Jeremy gave a heartfelt and very moving address. He had already told me that if there are indeed such things as Heaven and God, then Nanny will definitely be there 'sitting on the very right hand.'

Hopelessly tearful as is my wont at funerals, I was nonetheless happy that Nanny was here in her coffin rather than struggling with diminishing faculties in a hazy and lonely world, which she had probably been inhabiting for longer than she had wished. There is much to be said for vacating this life before it ceases to be worth living, but the goodbyes are nonetheless painful. Nanny had always been there for me, and I had depended on her for so much for so many years that the void would be great. I gave up the unequal struggle to sing, stared at the ceiling in an attempt to stem the tears and held tightly on to the proffered hand of Scarlett as she sat beside me. Talk about role reversal when a Granny has to rely on one so young. Kit conducted the service beautifully, as we all knew that he would. And considering that Mary Church had been one of his parishioners all those years ago, whom he had transported to functions of the Mothers Union on so many occasions, it seemed just right that he should be at the wheel for her final journey. As the service ended to the Nunc Dimittus, she was carried carefully out of the church to be re-loaded into the hearse awaiting her trip to the crematorium. I remembered how I had been told by Derek Gaskin, the funeral director, that although a cortege would appear to be travelling at funereal speed when approaching or leaving its destination, we should not be fooled. On reaching the open road a button could be pressed allowing a coffin to be released into the bowels of the hearse, whereupon the driver could 'step on it.' Furthermore, there was a capacity for two coffins to be transported at once, both of them out of sight for the duration of the journey. Thus whenever I see a supposedly empty hearse travelling at maximum speed along a motorway, the vision of the 'disappear the body' button springs to mind. Luckily there would be no motorways to be travelled between Heacham and King's Lynn, so presumably this particular hearse would park somewhere discreet for an hour or two before completing the rest of its journey.

Following the service we invited everyone to lunch in the Wheatsheaf pub opposite the church, where we had already made a previous visit to sample the fare and to book a room. It was a good choice. No one had to walk far, we could park cars in the forecourt and we could enjoy the interim period between the church service and the crematorium as we were treated to delicious Chilli Con Carne, trifle, cheese and coffee. We had anticipated that there would be plenty of takers for the bottles of wine, or even the beer, but we were wrong. We seemed to have no drinking drivers on this occasion and it was jugs of water, which were the preferred tipple.

At two o'clock a small number of us made our way to the crematorium at King's Lynn. Oh, the soulnessness of the place as one group of black clad people exited by one door, giving way to another group through another door. This then is the conveyor belt of death, and yet in many ways it seems a far better way of dispatching human remains than any other. This time we had the committing of the body to the furnace. As the button was pressed by Kit and the coffin disappeared, the finality of it all was in some ways comforting – to me at least. Imaginations can conjure up far worse images of the 'dust to dust' of the earth method of burial, than to the 'ashes to ashes' of the fire. I have never been partial to the 'worms shall consume them' thought.

Strangely, it was a happy day, which marked the end of what I hope was a happy life, within the limitations which fate had decreed for Mary Church. A pity she could not be there to enjoy once again the company of those she had once bounced on her knee, whose tears she had mopped up and with whom she had played hide and seek. Their being there with their various spouses was a tribute which she would never have expected, as one who 'didn't like to be a nuisance' but which would have made her very proud.

Chapter 16

A year has gone by since we said goodbye to Mary Church. The lovely old Georgian town of Swaffham is about to have a facelift, costing over six hundred thousand pounds. The traders of the famous Saturday market don't want it, nor do the shopkeepers or the residents. But the council in this politically correct world of ours have decreed that the money, much of it being our own taxes reclaimed back from the European Union, must be spent or relinquished. So they have appointed a 'partnership' as opposed to a 'quango' (it seems there's something distasteful about the word) to oversee 'the regeneration', which will include felling the plane trees, ill maintained but in their prime, limiting car parking, pedestrianising various streets and making a roundabout. New seats and flower tubs will be the added cosmetic niceties. Swaffham will be transformed and the resultant disruption and traffic jams will try everyone's patience, as well as jeopardising local trade. But for me, much as I dislike the plans, it may herald a new era. As it is, whenever I go past the turning to Hilton Court, I look to where I parked my bike on the wall outside, and I feel a sense of loss. Nanny look-alikes seem to abound, pushing shopping trolleys, just like the one she used for so long. Woolly hats pulled over white hair, padded jackets and sensible walking shoes are my reminders of someone whom I still miss terribly, about whom we still talk, who I hope DID find her real parents as well as her foster parents, somewhere 'out there.' I may not recall her so vividly when I encounter the armies of workmen in yellow helmets digging up the roads with their pneumatic drills. Nanny wouldn't have belonged here. She, who used to put her skipping rope on the ground so that a horse and cart could trot past, belonged to a gentler world before vandalism and political correctness became the modern scourge. She probably wouldn't have found her way so easily to our house either, pushing her chariot across all the fancy blocked paving that has been chosen for the makeover.

I hope that Heacham is not scheduled for regeneration. Mary Church was right to choose it for her final resting place. Her ashes were duly placed in the mound with her much loved foster family, and her name has been added to those already there. They are not in the manicured area surrounding the church, but rather in a somewhat wild and neglected field on the outskirts. But that would please Nanny. She was never one to be obtrusive and anyone looking for that particular grave will have difficulty finding it. The Rolfe and the Black families are also there, but in a special and somewhat grand enclosure. Visitors to the churchyard may see the graves and the carved inscriptions that have survived the ravages of the North Norfolk coastal weather, and are still readable. But they'll miss the stories that fashioned the lives of those that lie there. Graveyards guard their secrets just as Mary Church, the foundling, guarded hers.